The Publisher

S0-APQ-768

All instructional materials identified by the TAP® (Teachers/ Authors/Publishers) trademark are developed by a national network of teachers whose collective educational experience distinguishes the publishing objective of The Center for Learning, a nonprofit educational corporation founded in 1970.

Concentrating on values-related disciplines, The Center publishes humanities and religion curriculum units for use in public and private schools and other educational settings. Approximately 500 language arts, social studies, novel/drama, life issues, and faith publications are available.

While acutely aware of the challenges and uncertain solutions to growing educational problems, The Center is committed to quality curriculum development and to the expansion of learning opportunities for all students. Publications are regularly evaluated and updated to meet the changing and diverse needs of teachers and students. Teachers may offer suggestions for development of new publications or revisions of existing titles by contacting

The Center for Learning

Administrative/Editorial Office
21590 Center Ridge Road
Rocky River, Ohio, 44116
(440) 331-1404 • FAX (440) 331-5414
E-mail: cfl@stratos.net
Web: http://www.centerforlearning.org

For a free catalog containing order and price information and a descriptive listing of titles, contact

The Center for Learning

Shipping/Business Office
P.O. Box 910
Villa Maria, PA 16155
(724) 964-8083 • (800) 767-9090
FAX (888) 767-8080

Formula Writing Basics:
Beginning a Writing Proficiency Program

Janet Ehlert Cosner

 The Center for Learning

Janet Ehlert Cosner earned her B.S. in education from Kent State University, Kent, Ohio, and is pursuing an M.A. at Cleveland State University. She is a high school English teacher, the recipient of two Woodruff grants for writing, a Jennings scholar, and author of The Center for Learning's *Formula Writing 1—Building Toward Writing Proficiency* and *Formula Writing 2—Diverse Writing Situations.* Cosner is also listed in *Who's Who in American Teachers.*

The Publishing Team

Rose Schaffer, M.A., President/Chief Executive Officer
Bernadette Vetter, M.A., Vice President
Ellen Schuck, B.A., Coeditor
Amy Hollis, B.S.J., Coeditor

Cover Design

Krina K. Walsh, B.S.I.D.

Copyright © 1999 The Center for Learning.
Manufactured in the United States of America.

The worksheets in this book may be reproduced for academic purposes only and not for resale. Academic purposes refer to limited use within classroom and teaching settings only.

ISBN 1-56077-568-8

Contents

Introduction

Writing involves thinking, which is why it is so difficult for some students. Writing cannot be taught, but techniques that give students structure in writing can be taught. The formula method provides students with a way to begin and provides neophyte writers with a developmental process. Once students have studied traditional forms, they can develop their own structures and formulas. This book teaches the structure of many different kinds of essays; thus, students learn several ways to organize their thoughts and write well.

Although the formula program offers teachers a great deal of flexibility, the first nine lessons build on each other. The rest of the lessons teach specific structures for different writing assignments. Students learn how to use transitional words, adjectives, synonyms, figurative language, and onomatopoeia. They are taught how to make sentences longer and how to use grammar correctly. Interspersed in the lessons are creative exercises that allow the students to be imaginative. Writing charts for each assignment tell students the grading criteria for their papers. Teachers are encouraged to add specific objectives to the writing charts to meet the ability levels of the students.

The formula method is not meant to lock students into a set form but to be a starting point to help them organize their compositions. The formulas can change as students become more adept. The hope is that one day students will grow beyond them.

Teacher Notes

Rationale

Debates are swirling around the goals of the writing curriculums in our schools. Advocates of whole language techniques and the modern writing process are beginning to question the outcomes of their instruction. Isn't the end product more important than the process? Where do grammar and spelling fit in? Middle school and high school teachers complain that elementary students cannot communicate in writing. How can writing that is not only grammatically correct but also creative, logical, and thoughtful be taught? The formula method provides both structure and opportunity for creativity. The teaching of formulas, offering lessons in grammar and creativity, and clarifying the grading criteria by the use of a writing chart can motivate students to excellence in writing.

Using the Course Material

Formula Writing Basics consists of a teacher's manual of lesson plans and accompanying handouts. Lessons may be changed by altering the procedures, assignment requirements, or handout exercises to best suit student needs. For example, you may choose to change individual assignments to small group activities. Although the lessons should be taught in order, some of the lessons are optional. In particular, you may review and decide not to teach the portion of Lesson 5 that introduces the metaphor, a difficult concept for some children; Lesson 18, A Research Essay; or the portion of Lesson 19 that relies on research skills.

Lessons 1–9 include basic material suited for elementary students in grades 3–6; Lessons 10–19 teach more specific kinds of writing that may or may not be suited to students' ability levels. Lesson 20 expands on the proofreading process that is used throughout the unit.

Included in the book are formulas for a summary, a one-paragraph personal narrative essay, a one-paragraph fictional narrative essay, a friendly letter, journal writing, writing directions, book reports, interviews, a research essay, and speeches. Also included are grammar and creative exercises.

As part of their writing preparation, students are asked to complete "wheels." Drawing wheels on the board or making transparencies of the handouts will reinforce how students should complete them. Create wheel handouts on large sheets of paper to distribute to students if you find they require more space than that provided on the unit's handouts.

In Supplementary Materials, a generic wheel and writing chart are provided for teachers who choose to supplement or expand lessons by adding writing assignments. Also provided are pages that list the clustering and writing steps used throughout the unit. These pages can be made into transparencies or distributed to students for inclusion in their composition folders.

Throughout the unit, students may need to use their own paper to complete the exercises.

Student Notebooks

Each student should have a composition folder for important papers. A two-pocket folder with clips for paper in the center is recommended. Students should organize the folders by putting all formulas, lists, and charts in one pocket and essays that are finished or in progress in the other. The center section should be reserved for grammar notes and worksheets. By being organized, students will have all their writing tools at their fingertips.

Target Audience

The formula method in this unit was written for use with elementary students in grades three through six. However, it can be used with students of other grade levels and abilities, including learning disabled and special education children. The teacher who understands the ability levels of his or her students will have no trouble adapting formulas and exercises to a particular educational goal.

Writing Chart

An invaluable tool for both teachers and students, the writing chart lists all the requirements that students need to meet when they write an essay. Writing charts are always given to students before they begin writing. Once a lesson has been taught, the students are then held responsible for the content of the lesson. The chart can be made longer or shorter depending on the ability level of the class, but should get longer with each writing assignment.

As a teacher learns the students' ability levels, assignments can be given to clear up problem areas. These areas then can be added to the chart. Each chart has blank space so that other requirements may be added.

Another option is to add a column to the chart to allow a composition buddy (see below) to check that the chart requirements are met. If this practice is followed, the composition buddy can be graded or otherwise rewarded for a job well done.

Personal Dictionary

An activity that may benefit students is keeping a personal dictionary. At the beginning of the unit, instruct students to buy a three-ring notebook and label it with their names. Have each student insert twenty-six pieces of paper in the notebook, labeling each page with a letter from the alphabet. After each writing assignment is graded and returned, ask students to record any misspelled words on the proper page in their notebooks. Students may illustrate their dictionaries, but must allow room to record additional words.

Sharing

Most of the lessons end with the teacher sharing what the students have written. Students generally are thrilled to give permission for their papers to be read in class. Hearing their classmates' papers read aloud is an opportunity for students to know how their friends think and write.

Composition Buddies

Each student should have a composition buddy. Partners can change during the year so that students who have writing problems are teamed with students who write well. After students have written an essay, have the composition buddy read it to identify and correct mistakes. After both students have read each other's papers and corrected mistakes, they should complete the writing charts and attach them to their essays.

Lesson 20 requires students not only to proofread each other's papers as outlined here, but also to take more responsibility for the process by completing an evaluation form.

Grading

Put a check on the line of the student's paper where there is a mistake. If there is more than one mistake on a line, put as many checks as mistakes. When students get their essays back, they must find the mistakes and correct them. A revised paper could then be worth additional points. Grading the wheels students complete as part of their writing assignments may also be useful.

Lesson 1
A One-paragraph Essay

Objective

- To write a one-paragraph essay using the formula TS-6EX-SS (Topic Sentence—Six Examples—Summary Statement)

Notes to the Teacher

When you tell students to write a one-paragraph essay, they may not know how to begin, how many sentences they should write, or how long the sentences should be. With the formula method, students know exactly what is expected of them and have an easy way to express themselves.

The number of examples expected in the writing assignments can be changed to suit students' abilities. For example, a third grader might begin by writing a paragraph asking for only three examples (TS-3EX-SS).

Once students become comfortable with writing one-paragraph essays using the TS-6EX-SS formula, students can write about videos, short stories, novels, poems, or plays. Ask a question before reading or viewing and have the students cluster and write the essay.

To reinforce the formula, one-paragraph essays in other subject areas may be assigned while this lesson is taught.

In this lesson, students brainstorm, cluster ideas, and write one-paragraph essays. They use writing charts to be sure they have met specified writing requirements.

Procedure

1. Ask students what comes to mind when they think of ways to get physically fit. List students' ideas on the board. Let the ideas flow and write every idea down. Don't stop to judge.

   Explain to the students that starting with one idea and building on it is a prewriting technique called *brainstorming*. Brainstorming is often the most difficult part of writing.

2. Draw a wheel with six spokes on the board. As a class, choose six ideas from the list. Write the topic in the middle of the wheel on the board. Write each chosen idea on a spoke, called an inner spoke. The ideas do not have to be expressed in complete sentences. Tell the class that this is a cluster.

3. Distribute **Handout 1**. Ask students to complete the handout with the same information that is on the board.

   If the ability level of the students is low, see procedure 21.

4. Add spokes to the six inner spokes (see **Handout 2**). These are called the outer spokes, and are used to organize specific details that relate to the inner spokes.

   For example, if one of the answers on an inner spoke was "walking," the outer spoke might be a description of how far to walk in a certain time frame.

5. Allow class time for students to copy what is written on the board onto **Handout 2**. Have students complete the outer spokes on their own. Tell students that when the outer set of spokes is completed, it is time to write.

   To show students the importance of clustering before they write, **Handout 2** should be collected and graded.

6. Distribute **Handout 3** before students begin writing, so they will know exactly what is expected of them. You may choose to add other qualifications to the chart. As a class, review the writing chart. Tell students that when they complete a writing assignment, they should be sure they have met all of the requirements before putting a check mark in the student column and stapling the charts to their essays. Explain that you will return the writing chart with the essay after it is graded, with checks in the teacher column for items that are correct.

7. Begin writing the essay as a class. The teacher should write on the board and students should use their own paper. Use the words in the middle of the wheel to demonstrate how to write a topic sentence. Remind students to indent their paragraph.

8. The next step is writing a long, complete sentence for each spoke on the wheel. Tell students that to write long, complete sentences, they should combine the words on the inner spokes with the specific details on the outer spokes. Each spoke is made into a complete thought and a complete sentence.

You may direct the students to write these sentences on their own. However, be sure to set a sentence length (from at least six to eight words, depending on students' abilities) and explain that sentences begin with capital letters and end with punctuation marks.

9. The next step is writing a summary statement. Suggest to students that this sentence can be an opinion or a comment about the future. As a class, write a summary statement on the board. Students should add this sentence to the ends of the paragraphs on their papers.

10. Put the formula TS-6EX-SS on the board and explain what it means (Topic Sentence—Six Examples—Summary Sentence). (Remember to change the formula if you need to reflect a different number of example sentences.)

    Explain that students learned how to follow this formula when they wrote a topic sentence, six sentences using the inner and outer spokes on the wheel, and a summary sentence.

11. Assign a one-paragraph essay using the TS-6EX-SS formula. The topic is "My Favorite Things."

12. Distribute **Handout 4** and review the steps of clustering.

    - Write the topic of the essay in the middle of the wheel.
    - Brainstorm six related ideas for the inner spokes.
    - On the outer spokes, write details that support the examples on the inner spokes.

    Collect, grade, and return **Handout 4**.

13. Distribute **Handout 5** before students begin writing. Review how students are to use this handout (see procedure 6).

14. Direct students to begin writing their "My Favorite Things" essay. Remind them what the formula TS-6EX-SS means and how to use it.

- Use the words in the middle of the wheel to write a complete topic sentence.
- Combine the words on each inner spoke with the details on its outer spoke to write six long, complete sentences.
- Write a summary statement that contains an opinion or a comment about the future.

15. When students finish writing, tell them to complete the student column on **Handout 5**. When they are finished, they should staple **Handouts 4** and **5** to their essays and turn everything in for a grade.

16. Extend the lesson by asking students to use the formula to write descriptive paragraphs about the following topics. Simplify the topics or suggest different topics, depending on students' abilities.

    - Describe your favorite toy.
    - Describe your ideal car.
    - Describe how cities will change in the future.

17. Distribute **Handout 6**. Remind the students of the steps they should follow (see procedure 12). Collect, grade, and return **Handout 6**.

18. Distribute **Handout 7** before students begin to write. Review how students are to use this handout (see procedure 6).

19. Direct students to begin writing their essays. Remind the students of the steps they should follow (see procedure 14).

20. When students finish writing, tell them to complete the student column on **Handout 7**. When they are finished, they should staple **Handouts 6** and **7** to their essays and turn everything in for a grade.

21. If the ability level of the class is low, use **Handout 1** until the students can write short sentences using inner spokes only. Then introduce outer spokes (**Handout 2**) so that students can learn to add details to their sentences. The formula and writing chart are the same for both handouts.

Name_____

Date_____

A One-paragraph Essay Wheel

Directions: Write the topic in the middle of the wheel and fill the spokes with examples of your topic.

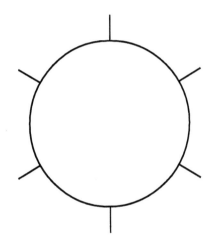

© COPYRIGHT, The Center for Learning. Used with permission. Not for resale.

3

Name_____

Date_____

A One-paragraph Detailed Essay Wheel

Directions: Write the topic in the middle of the wheel. Fill the inner spokes with examples of the topic. Then fill the outer spokes with details about the examples.

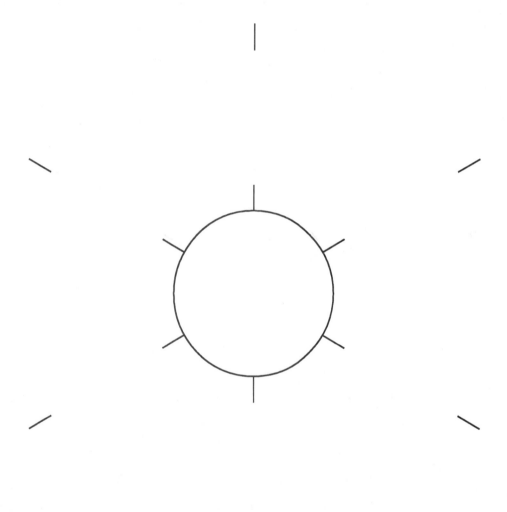

© COPYRIGHT, The Center for Learning. Used with permission. Not for resale.

Name_____

Date_____

Physically Fit Writing Chart

Directions: Before you turn in your paper, review this checklist to be sure you have met all the requirements. When you are sure of each item, put a check mark under the student column. Staple this chart to your paper. Your teacher will put check marks in the teacher column for what is correct.

Writing Checklist	Student	Teacher
Student indented the paragraph.		
Student followed the formula TS-6EX-SS.		
Student wrote complete sentences.		
Student used at least six to eight words in each sentence.		
Student capitalized the first letter of each sentence.		
Student used correct punctuation at the end of each sentence.		
Student checked spelling.		
Student reread the essay.		

© COPYRIGHT, The Center for Learning. Used with permission. Not for resale.

Name_____

Date_____

My Favorite Things Essay Wheel

Directions: Write the topic in the middle of the wheel. Fill the inner spokes with examples of the topic. Then fill the outer spokes with details about the examples on the inner spokes.

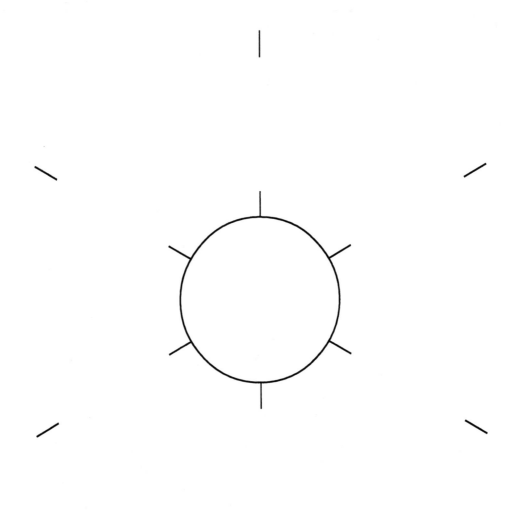

© COPYRIGHT, The Center for Learning. Used with permission. Not for resale.

My Favorite Things Writing Chart

Directions: Before you turn in your paper, review this checklist to be sure you have met all the requirements. When you are sure of each item, put a check mark under the student column. Staple this chart to your paper. Your teacher will put check marks in the teacher column for what is correct.

Writing Checklist	Student	Teacher
Student indented the paragraph.		
Student followed the formula TS-6EX-SS.		
Student wrote complete sentences.		
Student used at least six to eight words in a sentence.		
Student capitalized the first letter of each sentence.		
Student used correct punctuation at the end of each sentence.		
Student checked spelling.		
Student reread the paper.		

© COPYRIGHT. The Center for Learning. Used with permission. Not for resale.

Formula Writing Basics
Lesson 1
Handout 6

Name_____

Date_____

Description Essay Wheel

Directions: Write the topic in the middle of the wheel. Fill the inner spokes with examples of the topic. Then fill the outer spokes with specific details about the examples on the inner spokes.

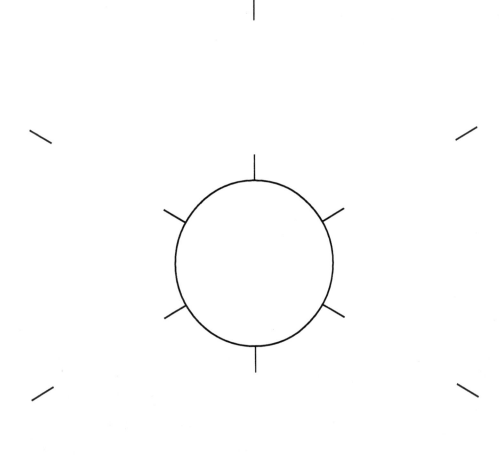

© COPYRIGHT, The Center for Learning. Used with permission. Not for resale.

Name_____

Date_____

Description Essay Writing Chart

Directions: Before you turn in your paper, review this checklist to be sure you have met all the requirements. When you are sure of each item, put a check mark under the student column. Staple this chart to your paper. Your teacher will put check marks in the teacher column for what is correct.

Writing Checklist	Student	Teacher
Student indented the paragraph.		
Student followed the formula TS-6EX-SS.		
Student wrote complete sentences.		
Student used at least six to eight words in a sentence.		
Student capitalized the first letter of each sentence.		
Student used correct punctuation at the end of each sentence.		
Student checked spelling.		
Student reread the essay.		

© COPYRIGHT, The Center for Learning. Used with permission. Not for resale.

Lesson 2
Transitional Words and Phrases

Objective
- To experience the necessity of using accurate transitional words

Notes to the Teacher
Most students begin their sentences with the same words. For example, they use *the* or *I* repeatedly. This "stuttering in writing" can be fixed by the use of transitional words that act as bridges from sentence to sentence. In a narrative paragraph, transitional words show chronological order. In a descriptive paragraph, they show spatial order. In an expository paragraph, they show the order of importance of the reasons and facts. By using transitional words, students make their papers more readable, organized, and precise.

In this lesson, students receive a list of transitional words and learn how different transitional words are used in different types of paragraphs. **Handout 8** demonstrates how a lack of transitional words makes reading and clarity difficult. Students add missing transitional words to a paragraph on **Handout 10**, write their own sentences with transitional words, and look for examples of transitional words in newspapers, magazines, or books. They close the lesson by using the TS-6EX-SS formula to write a paragraph with transitional words.

Procedure
1. Read **Handout 8** aloud to students. Ask them if anything seemed wrong with what you read. Try to lead students toward discovering that something was missing from what you read: transitional words that show order and connect ideas.

2. Distribute **Handout 9,** a list of transitional words and phrases. Explain that expository transitional words and phrases should be used in a paragraph that explains. Narrative transitional words should be used in a paragraph that is telling a story and descriptive transitional words should be used in a paragraph that is describing something. Students should keep **Handout 9** in their composition folders; this is the first of many lists that students will keep in these folders.

3. Distribute **Handout 8** and have students complete it. Review responses.

4. Distribute **Handout 10** and have students use **Handout 9** to complete the exercise. When students have finished, have them write a few sentences about a parade they have seen. Use **Handout 10** as a model. Instruct students to include at least three transitional words in their writing.

5. For additional practice, have students look for transitional words in a newspaper story, magazine article, or in a paragraph from a favorite book.

6. Extend the lesson by asking students to use the TS-6EX-SS formula and transitional words to write a paragraph on one of the following topics. Simplify the topics or suggest different topics depending on the ability level of your students.

   - Describe how things would change if you were in charge of the school.

   - Describe what kinds of music you like most and why.

   - Explain why you like to ride a skateboard.

7. Distribute **Handout 11** and remind students how to cluster.

   - Write the topic of the essay in the middle of the wheel.

   - Brainstorm six related ideas for the inner spokes.

   - On the outer spokes, write details that support the examples on the inner spokes.

   Collect, grade, and return **Handout 11** to students.

8. Distribute and review **Handout 12** before students begin writing. You may choose to add other qualifications to the chart. Establishing the following rule may be helpful:

   Students may not start more than two sentences with the same word. The third sentence must begin with a transitional word.

Tell students that when they complete the writing assignment, they should be sure they have met the requirements, put a check mark in the student column, and stapled the charts to their essays. Explain that you will return the writing chart with the paper after it is graded, with checks in the teacher column for items that are correct.

9. Tell students to take out their composition folders and to review their transitional words list (**Handout 9**).

10. As students begin writing, remind them what the formula TS-6EX-SS means (Topic Sentence—Six Examples— Summary Sentence) and how to use it.

    - Use the words in the middle of the wheel to write a complete topic sentence.

    - Combine the words on each inner spoke with the details on its outer spoke to write six long, complete sentences.

    - Write a summary statement that contains an opinion or a comment about the future.

11. When they are finished with their paragraphs, tell students to complete the student column on **Handout 12**. Then they should staple **Handouts 11** and **12** to their paragraphs and turn everything in for a grade.

Name_____

Date_____

Adding Transitional Words

Directions: Add transitional words to the following paragraphs to make them more exact and clear.

Race Car Driver

The race car driver stomped on the gas pedal. The car sped around the track. The driver reached a curve. Another car pulled out in front of him. The driver slammed on his brakes. His car hit the wall and turned over. An ambulance was called, and the emergency crew arrived. The driver was taken to the hospital where he had an operation on his leg. The driver went home later that week with one cast on his leg and one cast on his arm. His racing days were over.

Making a Hamburger

A hamburger is easy to make and tastes delicious. Divide the ground meat into equal parts, roll the parts into balls, and press the balls into flat pieces. Slowly brown the patties on a low flame until cooked. Take out ketchup, onion slices, lettuce, mustard, and a bun. Spread a layer of ketchup and mustard on the bun. Put the cooked hamburger patty on the bun. Place the lettuce and onion slices on top of the hamburger. Close the bun and enjoy your sandwich!

© COPYRIGHT, The Center for Learning. Used with permission. Not for resale.

Name_____

Date_____

Transitional Words and Phrases

Directions: Transitional words and phrases make your writing more exact. Use this list each time you write. Keep it in your folder and add any useful words or phrases as you learn them.

Expository	Narrative	Descriptive
afterward	first	above
later	then	alongside
next	finally	at the end of
then	soon	around
while	at the beginning	behind
following that	in the middle	below
the next step	by the time	down
the last step	eventually	near
also		
furthermore		

© COPYRIGHT, The Center for Learning. Used with permission. Not for resale.

Name_____

Date_____

Transitional Expressions

Directions: Use transitional words from **Handout 9** to fill in the blanks.

The Fourth of July Parade

Each year I look forward to the best parade of the year, the Fourth of July parade. _____

the band comes into view, and I can already feel the excitement of the crowd. _____

the music begins, and I can feel my feet beginning to dance. _____ the marching band

come the floats. _____ are decorated cars full of important political people.

_____ come the tumbling clowns throwing candy to the crowd. _____

are the brightly colored floats decorated with flags and other patriotic symbols. Every year I can't wait

to see this parade!

© COPYRIGHT, The Center for Learning. Used with permission. Not for resale.

Formula Writing Basics
Lesson 2
Handout 11

Name_____

Date_____

Transitional Words Detailed Essay Wheel

Directions: Write the topic in the middle of the wheel. Fill the inner spokes with examples of the topic. Then fill the outer spokes with specific details about the examples on the inner spokes.

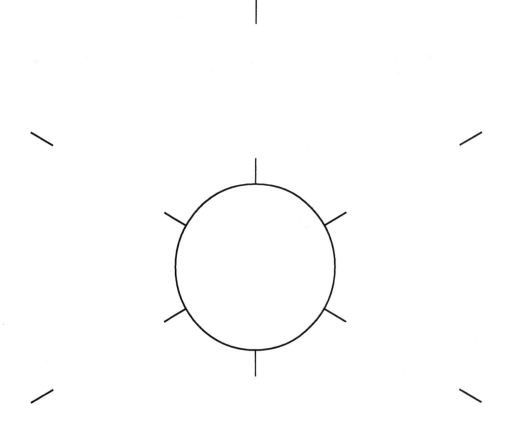

© COPYRIGHT, The Center for Learning. Used with permission. Not for resale.

Transitional Words Essay Writing Chart

Directions: Before you turn in your paper, review this checklist to be sure you have met all the requirements. When you are sure of each item, put a check mark under the student column. Staple this chart to your paper. Your teacher will put check marks in the teacher column for what is correct.

Writing Checklist	Student	Teacher
Student indented the paragraph.		
Student followed the formula TS-6EX-SS.		
Student used one transitional word.		
Student wrote complete sentences.		
Student used at least six to eight words in a sentence.		
Student capitalized the first letter of each sentence.		
Student used correct punctuation at the end of each sentence.		
Student checked spelling.		
Student reread the essay.		

© COPYRIGHT. The Center for Learning. Used with permission. Not for resale.

Lesson 3
Sensory Experiences

Objective

• To enliven writing through translation of sensory experiences

Notes to the Teacher

Students are not always aware of their surroundings. As writers, they must become sensitive to sensations all around them and use precise words to describe their environment. To become an expert observer requires training in how to use all five senses and how to communicate what is experienced. As students practice describing their sensory reactions, they become more cognizant of the world and their writing becomes more vivid and exact.

In this lesson, students study a list of sensory adjectives, define adjective, and practice using sensory adjectives. Students review the TS-6EX-SS formula by writing a paragraph with sensory adjectives.

Procedure

1. Ask students to describe the following:

   • the sight of a rainbow
   • the taste of a pizza
   • the scent of a fire
   • the sound of a car horn
   • the texture of sandpaper

2. Ask students what kinds of words they are using to describe these items. As needed, review the definition of adjective. Tell students that sensory adjectives are descriptive words that relate to the five senses.

3. Distribute **Handout 13**. Show the class how the list of sensory adjectives is divided into the five senses: sight, taste, smell, sound, and touch. Tell students to keep this handout in their composition folders.

4. Tell the students that the sensory adjectives on **Handout 13** can help a writer create a "picture image" for a reader. Explain that this means that a writer can describe almost exactly the way something looks by using sight adjectives. Sound, touch, taste, and smell adjectives also help writers describe things. Ask students to refer to words

in the appropriate areas of **Handout 13** to describe the following:

1. the look of the sky
2. the taste of a cookie
3. the smell of food in the lunchroom
4. the appearance of a friend
5. the sound of a siren
6. the feel of a cat
7. the sound of a sister or brother
8. the feel of liver
9. the taste of liver
10. the smell of a gym locker

5. Ask students to use their five senses to describe the following:

   1. a toothbrush
   2. a hairdo
   3. a purse
   4. the morning sky
   5. potato chips
   6. a baby's face

6. Distribute **Handout 14** and have students use **Handout 13** to complete it. Remind students that each sentence should contain two sensory adjectives. Share the best papers with the class.

7. Instruct the students to work in pairs to make a list of adjectives to describe an object or place familiar to all the students. Possible choices:
   • the gym
   • the cafeteria
   • a grocery store
   • a park
   • a mall
   • your city

   The student pair who has the longest list could be rewarded.

8. Instruct students to look in a book, magazine, or newspaper for adjectives. Discuss how the adjectives add sharp sensory detail to the passages found.

9. Distribute **Handout 15** and read the paragraph aloud. Explain to students that the paragraph contains a lot of adjectives. Tell the students to cross out all the adjectives and to read the changed paragraph. Then discuss with students the importance of adjectives and what happened to the paragraph when the adjectives were removed. Discuss what happens when adjectives are not used in writing.

10. Extend the lesson by asking students to use the TS-6EX-SS formula and sensory adjectives to write a paragraph on one of the following topics. Simplify the topics or suggest different topics depending on the ability level of your students.

    - Tell at whose house you would like to be a guest and why.

    - Explain the ways that you are creative.

    - Describe what you would do if you were president of the United States.

    - Describe what you like most about school.

11. Distribute **Handout 16** and remind students how to cluster.

    - Write the topic of the essay in the middle of the wheel.

    - Brainstorm six related ideas for the inner spokes.

    - On the outer spokes, write details that support the examples on the inner spokes.

    Collect, grade, and return **Handout 16** to students.

12. Before students begin writing, distribute **Handout 17** and review it. You may choose to add other qualifications to the chart. Tell students that when they complete the writing assignment, they should be sure they have met the requirements, put a check mark in the student column, and stapled the charts to their essays. Explain that you will return the writing chart with the paper after it is graded, with checks in the teacher column for items that are correct.

13. Tell students to take out their composition folders and to review their lists of transitional words (**Handout 9**) and sensory adjectives (**Handout 13**).

14. As students begin writing, remind them what the formula TS-6EX-SS means (Topic Sentence—Six Examples—Summary Sentence) and how to use it.

    - Use the words in the middle of the wheel to write a complete topic sentence.

    - Combine the words on each inner spoke with the details on its outer spoke to write six long, complete sentences.

    - Write a summary statement that contains an opinion or a comment about the future.

15. When they are finished with their paragraphs, tell students to complete the student column on **Handout 17**. Then they should staple **Handouts 16** and **17** to their paragraphs and turn everything in for a grade.

Sensory Adjectives

Directions: The adjectives listed here describe what we see, hear, touch, taste, and smell. These words help writers describe things. Use this list each time you write. Keep it in your folder and add useful words as you learn them.

Sight	Shape	Colors	Sound	Touch	Taste
large	flat	*Red*	booming	cool	spicy
gigantic	square	cherry	stomping	sticky	sugary
pretty	crooked	tomato	exploding	damp	bitter
chubby	narrow	ruby	banging	fuzzy	salty
fluffy	circular	raspberry	crashing	greasy	sour
glamorous	rotund	*Blue*	harsh	slippery	bland
homely	straight	royal	rumbling	frosty	oily
pale	curved	aqua	screaming	feathery	creamy
clean	wavy	navy	screeching	cold	hot
bright	forked	turquoise	snarling	hairy	juicy
skinny	rectangular	*Black*	humming	cool	strong
spotless	gigantic	tar	swishing	rubbery	tasteless
ugly	long	licorice	murmuring	dirty	buttery
tall	oval	jet	buzzing	velvety	
filthy	bent	*Gray*	cooing	dusty	**Smell**
dark	square	pearl	crackling	bumpy	minty
shiny		silver	gurgling	gooey	spicy
glassy		steel	hissing	icy	fishy
cheap		*Yellow*	purring	hot	burnt
muddy		gold	quiet	hard	moldy
dull		butter-	rustling	sharp	sweet
old		scotch	whimpering	silky	fragrant
used		canary	whispering	tender	smoky
worn		lemon	sighing	warm	stinky
shabby		butter		smooth	sour
big		*White*	bellowing	sweaty	fresh
bulky		cream	screaming	wet	clean
colorful		chalk	howling	slimy	perfumed
deep		snowy	growling	sandy	
elegant		milky	giggling	coarse	
fancy		*Brown*	barking		
foggy		rust	groaning		
high		tan	shrieking		
misty		chocolate	squealing		
shy		walnut	whistling		
sunny		*Green*	squawking		
spotless		emerald	chattering		
small		celery	stammering		
		mint	stuttering		
		lime			
		olive			
		Purple			
		orchid			
		grape			
		violet			

© COPYRIGHT, The Center for Learning. Used with permission. Not for resale.

Name_____

Date_____

Sense Sentences

Directions: Use **Handout 13** to write complete sentences that describe the following items. Each sentence should use two sensory adjectives. Check your sentences for correct spelling and grammar.

1. the playground

2. a forkful of spaghetti

3. a girl's eyes

4. a snowstorm

5. the school hall

6. a basketball

7. cotton candy

8. a wet cat

9. a toy

10. popcorn

11. a fish

12. a bike

13. candy

14. a video game

15. a mall

© COPYRIGHT, The Center for Learning. Used with permission. Not for resale.

Using Adjectives

Directions: Follow your teacher's instructions to complete this activity.

Sunday Dinner

I love Sunday dinner in our family. Everyone in the entire family gathers around the large kitchen table. The five of us sit there for hours, eating and talking. The shiny, long table is jammed with plates of buttery mashed potatoes, thick crisp green beans, juicy fried chicken, and hot biscuits. From one corner of the room drifts the strong, rich aroma of coffee mixed with the sweet smell of warm apple pie. When we leave the table, we all head straight to our warm, cozy beds for an afternoon nap!

© COPYRIGHT, The Center for Learning. Used with permission. Not for resale.

Name_____

Date_____

Sensory Adjectives Detailed Essay Wheel

Directions: Write the topic in the middle of the wheel. Fill the inner spokes with examples of the topic. Then fill the outer spokes with specific details about the examples on the inner spokes.

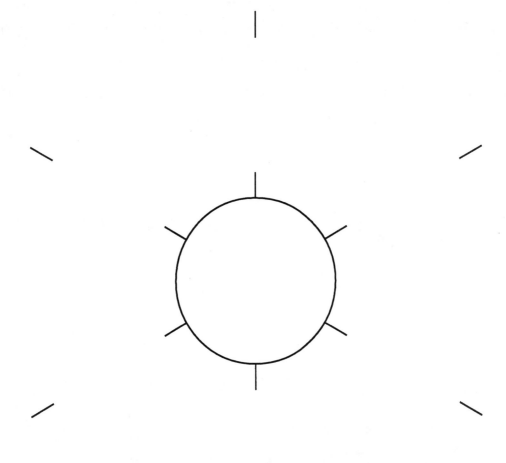

© COPYRIGHT, The Center for Learning. Used with permission. Not for resale.

Name_____

Date_____

Sensory Adjectives Essay Writing Chart

Directions: Before you turn in your paper, review this checklist to be sure you have met all the requirements. When you are sure of each item, put a check mark under the student column. Staple this chart to your paper. Your teacher will put check marks in the teacher column for what is correct.

Writing Checklist	Student	Teacher
Student indented the paragraph.		
Student followed the formula TS-6EX-SS.		
Student used one transitional word.		
Student used two adjectives.		
Student wrote complete sentences.		
Student used at least six to eight words in a sentence.		
Student capitalized the first letter of each sentence.		
Student used correct punctuation at the end of each sentence.		
Student checked spelling.		
Student reread the essay.		

© COPYRIGHT, The Center for Learning. Used with permission. Not for resale.

Lesson 4
Synonyms

Objective
- To find words that best communicate an idea

Notes to the Teacher

Students tend to repeat the same words in their essays. For example, if an essay is about a parent, students will use the word *parent* fifteen times. Before students write, have them make a list of the words they will be using often in their essay. Then instruct them to look up those words in a thesaurus so that their essays will not "stutter" with the same words. Remind students that the differences in meaning among synonyms are of critical importance. Before they use a synonym, they should check its full meaning in a dictionary. By finding the exact words for their meanings, students will add variety and precision to their writing.

Students will need a thesaurus for this and subsequent lessons. If there are none available in the classroom, students may need to bring one from home or buy one.

Depending on the ability level of the students, you may need to review what nouns, verbs, adjectives, prefixes, and suffixes are before beginning this lesson. You may also need to take some class time to carefully explain what synonyms are. Begin the lesson when you are satisfied that students understand these terms.

In this lesson, students use a thesaurus to find synonyms and are introduced to a synonym chart that they will use in future writing assignments. Students also review the TS-6EX-SS formula by writing a paragraph with synonyms.

Procedure

1. Ask students to make a list of five or ten words that are synonyms of *pretty;* no slang is allowed. Most students will have some trouble with this exercise. Ask them to come up with five synonyms for the word *girl.* This also will not be easy for them. Try a verb, such as *run.* What students soon discover is their vocabularies are not extensive and that they could use some help in finding synonyms to provide variety and exactness in their writing.

2. Point out to students that you have given them an adjective, *pretty;* a noun, *girl;* and a verb, *run.* Tell them that a thesaurus is a book that can help them find synonyms for these words. Explain that they will need a thesaurus for this and following lessons to help them find words to use when they write. Mention that buying a thesaurus is a good investment if they do not already have access to one.

3. Demonstrate how to use the thesaurus by having students look up the word *danger.* Point out that by using the thesaurus they will learn that danger, a noun, has many synonyms that may offer the exact meaning for which they are searching. Also, point out that danger can become a verb or an adjective by the additions of prefixes and suffixes (*endanger* is a verb; *dangerous* is an adjective). Synonyms also exist for the verb and adjective forms of the words. Lastly, show students the "See Also" section, where they can find similar words that may be more exact. Sometimes students will not be able to find the word they are looking for in the thesaurus. Point out that they may have to look up a form of the word they want instead of the actual word.

4. Explain that students now need to refer to the lists of transitional words and sensory adjectives in their composition folders and a thesaurus when they write. Explain that a new requirement will be added to the writing chart when they next use it: Students may not repeat the same noun, adjective, or verb more than three times in an essay.

5. Assign **Handout 18** for initial thesaurus use. As a class, review the synonyms students found.

6. Make several copies of **Handout 19** for each student. Students should keep these pages in their composition folders. Tell students that before they begin any future writing assignment, they should complete this handout.

27

7. Extend the lesson by asking students to write paragraphs about one of the following topics using the TS-6EX-SS formula and synonyms. Simplify the topics or suggest different ones depending on the ability level of your students.

   - Describe something you did last summer.
   - Explain why you would or would not like to travel in space.
   - Describe your favorite cartoon character.
   - Describe what you would do if you knew how to drive and had a car.

8. Distribute **Handout 20** and remind students how to cluster.

   - Write the topic of the essay in the middle of the wheel.
   - Brainstorm six related ideas for the inner spokes.
   - On the outer spokes, write details that support the examples on the inner spokes.

   Collect, grade, and return **Handout 20** to students.

9. Before students begin writing, distribute **Handout 21** and review it. You may choose to add other qualifications to the chart. Tell students that when they complete the writing assignment, they should be sure they have met the requirements of each item on the chart, put a check mark in the student column, and stapled the charts to their essays. Explain that you will return the writing chart with the paper after it is graded, with checks in the teacher column for items that are correct.

10. Have students review their transitional words and sensory adjectives lists. Direct them to complete a synonym chart (**Handout 19**), which they should have in their composition folders.

11. As students begin writing, remind them what the formula TS-6EX-SS (Topic Sentence—Six Examples—Summary Sentence) means and how to use it.

    - Use the words in the middle of the wheel to write a complete topic sentence.
    - Combine the words on each inner spoke with the details on its outer spoke to write six long, complete sentences.
    - Write a summary statement that contains an opinion or a comment about the future.

12. When they are finished with their paragraphs, tell students to complete the student column on **Handout 21**. Then they should staple **Handouts 19**, **20**, and **21** to their essays and turn everything in for a grade.

Name_____

Date_____

Synonyms—Nouns, Adjectives, and Verbs

Directions: Look up the following words in a thesaurus. Find at least ten synonyms for each word.

1. dress

2. house

3. friend

4. dog

5. teacher

6. drink

7. walk

8. see

9. talk

10. play

11. angry

12. ugly

13. big

14. skinny

15. happy

© COPYRIGHT, The Center for Learning. Used with permission. Not for resale.

Name_____

Date_____

Synonym Chart

Directions: Before you write, make a list of the words you will use often in your essay. Write one word at the top of each column. Use a thesaurus and a dictionary to help you find synonyms for the words. Write the synonyms in the columns below each word. Use these synonyms in your essay.

© COPYRIGHT, The Center for Learning. Used with permission. Not for resale.

Name_____

Date_____

Synonyms Detailed Essay Wheel

Directions: Write the topic in the middle of the wheel. Fill the inner spokes with examples of the topic. Then fill the outer spokes with specific details about the examples on the inner spokes.

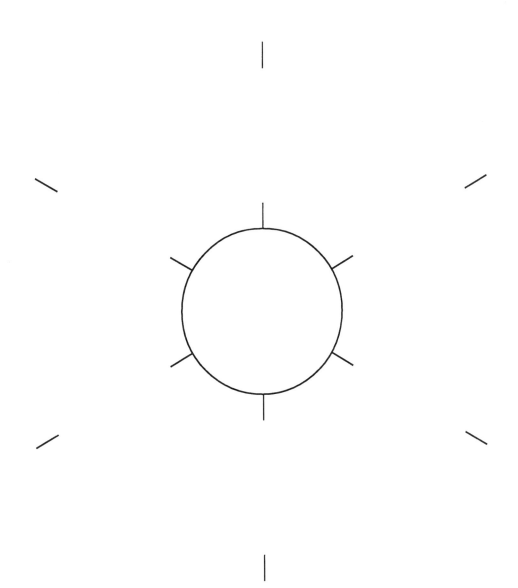

© COPYRIGHT, The Center for Learning. Used with permission. Not for resale.

Formula Writing Basics
Lesson 4
Handout 21

Name_____

Date_____

Synonyms Essay Writing Chart

Directions: Before you turn in your paper, review this checklist to be sure you have met all the requirements. When you are sure of each item, put a check mark under the student column. Staple this chart to your paper. Your teacher will put check marks in the teacher column for what is correct.

Writing Checklist	Student	Teacher
Student indented the paragraph.		
Student followed the formula TS-6EX-SS.		
Student used one transitional word.		
Student used two adjectives.		
Student used synonyms.		
Student did not repeat the same noun, adjective, or verb more than three times.		
Student wrote complete sentences.		
Student used at least six to eight words in a sentence.		
Student capitalized the first letter of each sentence.		
Student used correct punctuation at the end of each sentence.		
Student checked spelling.		
Student reread the essay.		

© COPYRIGHT, The Center for Learning. Used with permission. Not for resale.

Lesson 5
Figurative Language

Objective
- To correctly use metaphor, simile, and personification

Notes to the Teacher
Unless a reader can connect a word with an object or concept, it has no meaning. A writer must be able to create a mental picture for the reader. This can be accomplished by using metaphors or similes to compare an object or concept with something that the reader already knows. The use of personification adds a different twist to students' writing by creating unusual pictures in the reader's mind. By using these figures of speech, students tap into their creativity and show readers a new way to look at something. The goal of the lesson is to get students to think in pictures and to visualize what is being described.

Depending on the ability level of your students, you may choose not to teach the portion of this lesson that introduces the metaphor, which is a difficult concept for some students. You also may choose to reinforce the material presented in this lesson with exercises from composition or grammar textbooks.

In this lesson, students define metaphor, simile, cliché, and personification; participate in classroom discussions; and create their own metaphors, similes, and personification. They also review the TS-6EX-SS formula by writing a paragraph containing the literary devices introduced in the lesson.

Procedure
1. Write the following statements on the board.

   He was a lion in the classroom.

   Winter is a dark tunnel.

   Ask students: Was a lion really in the classroom? Is winter really a dark tunnel through which someone can walk or drive?

   Lead students to the conclusion that these statements aren't really true. Tell students that each sentence contains a *metaphor*, a comparison of two unlike things.

2. Distribute **Handout 22** and have students complete it. Share responses in a class discussion.

3. Write the following on the board:

   Her eyes flashed like lightning.

   The boy climbed as effortlessly as a monkey.

   The wind howled like a wounded dog.

   Ask students: Did lightning bolts really flash in a girl's eyes? Did a boy really use a tail and claws to climb, or swing upside down on branches like a monkey would? Did the wind really howl just like a wounded dog?

   Lead students to the conclusion that these statements really aren't true. Tell students that the sentences each contain *similes*, a comparison of two unlike things using the words *like* or *as*.

4. Write the following on the board:

   Joe was as fit as a fiddle.

   The man was as dumb as an ox.

   Ask students: Was Joe really as fit as a fiddle, with his strings in tune and tightened properly? Could a man really be as dumb as an ox, knowing only where it gets its food and water and nothing else?

   Lead students to the conclusion that these statements really aren't true. Tell students that the sentences each contain a *cliché*, an expression or idea that has been used so often that it has lost its effectiveness. Ask students if they can think of other clichés.

5. Distribute **Handout 23** and have students complete it. Share the best answers with the class.

6. Ask students to illustrate some of the similes they wrote on **Handout 23.** Tell students to be creative. Display the illustrations in the classroom.

7. Write the following on the board:

    The sky cried on the sad day.

    The flower smiled at the sun.

    The tree danced merrily.

    Ask students: Can the sky really cry when something sad happens? Can a flower really smile at the sun or be happy? Can a tree really dance?

    Lead students to the conclusion that these statements really aren't true. Tell students that the sentences contain examples of *personification*, giving an idea, place, or object a personality or personal attribute. Ask students to explain what is personified in the sentences on the board. (*The sky, the flower, and the tree are personified. The sky can't cry, the flower can't smile, and the tree can't dance.*)

8. Have students complete **Handout 24**. Students will see that by using this technique their writing will create unusual pictures in the reader's mind. Read the best answers to the class.

9. Extend the lesson by asking students to write paragraphs about one of the following topics using the TS-6EX-SS formula and a simile or metaphor. Simplify the topics or suggest different ones depending on the ability level of your students.

    *   If you had six wishes today, what would they be?

    *   Describe your best friend.

    *   If you had x-ray vision, describe an adventure you might have.

10. Distribute **Handout 25** and remind students how to cluster.

    *   Write the topic of the essay in the middle of the wheel.

    *   Brainstorm six related ideas for the inner spokes.

    *   On the outer spokes, write details that support the examples on the inner spokes.

    Collect, grade, and return **Handout 25** to students.

11. Before students begin writing, distribute **Handout 26** and review it. You may choose to add other qualifications to the chart. Tell students that when they complete the writing assignment, they should be sure they have met the requirements of each item on the chart, put a check mark in the student column, and stapled the charts to their essays. Explain that you will return the writing chart with the paper after it is graded, with checks in the teacher column for items that are correct.

12. Have students review their lists of transitional words and sensory adjectives. Direct them to complete a synonym chart (**Handout 19**), which they should have in their composition folders. As students begin to write, remind them what the formula TS-6EX-SS means (Topic Sentence—Six Examples—Summary Sentence) and how to use it.

    *   Use the words in the middle of the wheel to write a complete topic sentence.

    *   Combine the words on each inner spoke with the details on its outer spoke to write six long, complete sentences.

    *   Write a summary statement that contains an opinion or a comment about the future.

13. When they are finished with their paragraphs, tell students to complete the student column on **Handout 26**. Then they should staple **Handouts 19**, **25**, and **26** to their paragraphs and turn everything in for a grade.

Name_____

Date_____

Metaphors

Directions: Create metaphors that compare the item to something else. Try to think of unusual comparisons. Then use your metaphor in a long, complete sentence.

1. the moon

2. the fox

3. the sun

4. the car

5. the wagon

6. the TV

7. the radio

8. the bike

9. the skateboard

10. the clouds

© COPYRIGHT, The Center for Learning. Used with permission. Not for resale.

Name_____

Date_____

Similes

Directions: Complete the following similes. Remember that a simile is a comparison of two unlike things that uses the words *like* or *as.* Then write a long, complete sentence using each simile.

1. as red as

2. cold like

3. as smooth as

4. slow like

5. as soft as

6. loud like

7. as flat as

8. sweet like

9. as stale as

10. as bright as

© COPYRIGHT, The Center for Learning. Used with permission. Not for resale.

Name_____

Date_____

Personification

Directions: Write sentences using personification to describe the objects below.

1. a desk

2. a TV

3. a car

4. a bike

5. a plane

6. a garden

7. a doll

8. a wagon

9. a dog

10. a plate

© COPYRIGHT, The Center for Learning. Used with permission. Not for resale.

Name_____

Date_____

Metaphor and Simile Detailed Essay Wheel

Directions: Write the topic in the middle of the wheel. Fill the inner spokes with examples of the topic. Then fill the outer spokes with specific details about the examples on the inner spokes.

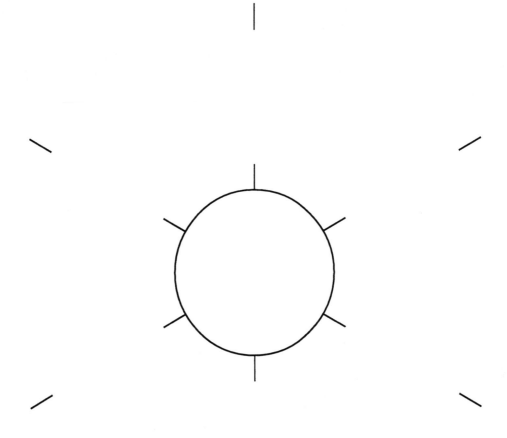

© COPYRIGHT, The Center for Learning. Used with permission. Not for resale.

Name_____

Date_____

Metaphor and Simile Essay Writing Chart

Directions: Before you turn in your paper, review this checklist to be sure you have met all the requirements. When you are sure of each item, put a check mark under the student column. Staple this chart to your paper. Your teacher will put check marks in the teacher column for what is correct.

Writing Checklist	Student	Teacher
Student indented the paragraph.		
Student followed the formula TS-6EX-SS.		
Student used one transitional word.		
Student used one simile or metaphor.		
Student used two adjectives.		
Student used synonyms.		
Student did not repeat the same noun, adjective, or verb more than three times.		
Student wrote complete sentences.		
Student used at least six to eight words in a sentence.		
Student capitalized the first letter of each sentence.		
Student used correct punctuation at the end of each sentence.		
Student checked spelling.		
Student reread the essay.		

© COPYRIGHT, The Center for Learning. Used with permission. Not for resale.

Lesson 6
Onomatopoeia

Objective
- To define and practice onomatopoeia in writing

Notes to the Teacher
The use of onomatopoeia gives students' writing a different twist. Adding this technique to students' repertoire of writing tools provides uniqueness and sound. The reader will be surprised by this fresh and original way of writing and the writer will have fun incorporating onomatopoeia into his or her expression. Effective use of sound words can enhance the imagery and realism of writing.

In this lesson, students learn what onomatopoeia is and use it in their writing. Students find examples of onomatopoeia in magazines, on television, and in newspapers. Finally, students review the formula TS-6EX-SS by writing an essay with onomatopoeia words.

Procedure
1. Write the following phrases on the board:

   the swish of the broom

   the bang of the drum

   the crack of the whip

   the bus whizzed by

   the alarm clock's buzz

   Have student volunteers read each of the phrases aloud. Then read aloud the following phrases:

   the sound of the broom

   the noise of the drum

   the sound of the whip

   the bus going by

   the alarm clock's sound

   Ask students what the difference is between the phrases on the board and the phrases that you read aloud. Lead them into deciding that the phrases on the board are more descriptive and interesting than the phrases you read.

2. Explain to students that *onomatopoeia* is using words that sound like what they mean, and that the phrases on the board are examples of onomatopoeia. Tell the class that these words are very expressive and add sound effects to writing.

3. Distribute **Handout 27**. Ask students to share with the class any onomatopoeia words they can add to the list. Have students keep this handout in their composition folders.

4. Distribute **Handout 28** and have students complete it. Read the best answers aloud in class.

5. Distribute **Handout 29** and have students complete it. Share the best responses with the class.

6. Have students find examples of onomatopoeia in magazines, on television, and in newspapers. Make a bulletin board of the best examples.

7. Extend the lesson by asking students to write paragraphs about one of the following topics using the TS-6EX-SS formula and an onomatopoeia word. Simplify the topics or suggest different ones depending on the ability level of your students.

   - Describe how you think the world will be different in twenty years.
   - Describe what your ideal restaurant would be like.
   - Describe a concert.

8. Distribute **Handout 30**. Remind students how to cluster.

   - Write the topic of the essay in the middle of the wheel.
   - Brainstorm six related ideas for the inner spokes.
   - On the outer spokes, write details that support the examples on the inner spokes.

   Collect, grade, and return **Handout 30.**

9. Distribute and review **Handout 31** before students begin writing. You may choose to add other qualifications to the chart. Tell students that when they complete the writing assignment, they should be sure they have met the requirements of each item on the chart, put a check mark in the student column, and stapled the charts to their essays. Explain that you will return the writing chart with the paper after it is graded, with checks in the teacher column for items that are correct.

10. Tell students to review their lists of transitional words, sensory adjectives, and onomatopoeia words. Direct them to complete a synonym chart (**Handout 19**), which they should have in their composition folders.

11. As students begin writing, remind them what the formula TS-6EX-SS means (Topic Sentence—Six Examples—Summary Sentence) and how to use it.

   • Use the words in the middle of the wheel to write a complete topic sentence.

   • Combine the words on each inner spoke with the details on its outer spoke to write six long, complete sentences.

   • Write a summary statement that contains an opinion or a comment about the future.

12. When they are finished with their paragraphs, tell students to complete the student column on **Handout 31**. Then they should staple **Handouts 19**, **30**, and **31** to their paragraphs and turn everything in for a grade.

Name_____

Date_____

Onomatopoeia Words

Directions: The words below are onomatopoeia words. Add words to the list as you think of them.

bang	cough	moo	splash
beep	crack	neigh	squeak
boom	creak	plop	swish
buzz	crunch	pop	tick
chirp	drip	ring	thud
clack	fizz	roar	thump
clang	growl	rustle	tinkle
clatter	grunt	screech	whack
click	hiss	shriek	whiz
clink	honk	sizzle	whoop
clomp	hum	snort	zip
coo	meow	smash	zoom
cuckoo			

© COPYRIGHT, The Center for Learning. Used with permission. Not for resale.

Name_____

Date_____

Onomatopoeia Sentences

Directions: Write long, complete sentences using the words below with onomatopoeia words.

1. airplane

2. mother

3. computer

4. lunchroom

5. playground

6. fire engine

7. amusement ride

8. car race

9. parade

10. dryer

© COPYRIGHT, The Center for Learning. Used with permission. Not for resale.

Name_____

Date_____

More Sound Words

Directions: Make up your own onomatopoeia words that describe the following items. Then write long, complete sentences that include your new words. When you use a made-up word, put the word in quotation marks.

1. a stream

2. hot dogs on a grill

3. wind blowing

4. a train

5. a cat running on piano keys

6. shoes on a tile floor

7. a shrill voice

8. a washing machine

9. rain on a roof

10. police car siren

© COPYRIGHT, The Center for Learning. Used with permission. Not for resale.

Name_____

Date_____

Onomatopoeia Detailed Essay Wheel

Directions: Write the topic in the middle of the wheel. Fill the inner spokes with examples of the topic. Then fill the outer spokes with specific details about the examples on the inner spokes.

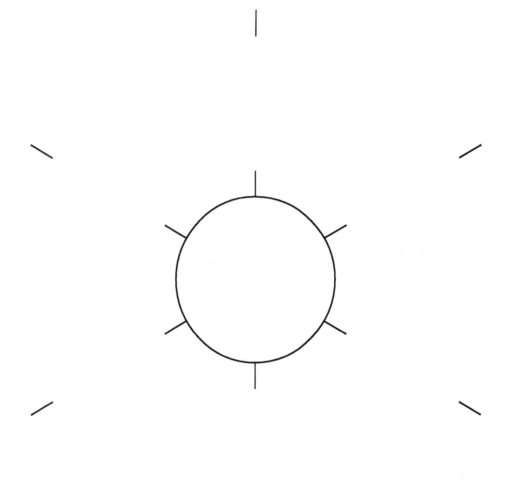

© COPYRIGHT, The Center for Learning. Used with permission. Not for resale.

Name_____

Date_____

Onomatopoeia Essay Writing Chart

Directions: Before you turn in your paper, review this checklist to be sure you have met all the requirements. When you are sure of each item, put a check mark under the student column. Staple this chart to your paper. Your teacher will put check marks in the teacher column for what is correct.

Writing Checklist	Student	Teacher
Student indented the paragraph.		
Student followed the formula TS-6EX-SS.		
Student used one transitional word.		
Student used one simile or metaphor.		
Student used two adjectives.		
Student used one onomatopoeia word.		
Student used synonyms.		
Student did not repeat the same noun, adjective, or verb more than three times.		
Student wrote complete sentences.		
Student used at least six to eight words in a sentence.		
Student capitalized the first letter of each sentence.		
Student used correct punctuation at the end of each sentence.		
Student checked spelling.		
Student reread the essay.		

© COPYRIGHT, The Center for Learning. Used with permission. Not for resale.

Lesson 7
Creativity

Objective

- To think and write creatively

Notes to the Teacher

Structure is very important in writing. That is why formula writing is so successful. But within the structure of the paragraph, students can be creative. By using their imaginations, students can write original and creative essays.

Although students sometimes feel that their creativity has been stifled, completing the following exercises will help students to recognize and express their uniqueness. If you read the best work aloud to the class, students will be surprised at how creative they really can be.

In this lesson, students focus on creativity during brainstorming activities and essay writing.

Procedure

1. To warm up students' imaginations, brainstorm with them a few minutes each day about a topic of your choice. Ask students to write quickly about the topic in a creative way. Possible topics:

   - Describe a dream.

   - If your home was on fire, what five things would you take to safety?

   - What would the perfect parents be like?

   - What is something you learned in life so far?

   - Describe your pet.

   Another brainstorming activity is introducing a topic and asking students to list related items aloud or in writing as quickly as they can. Push students to make longer lists every time you lead this type of session. Possible topics:

   - movies

   - sports

   - holidays

   - animals

   - cars

   Students find these exercises fun and soon let their imaginations soar. Whatever type of brainstorming exercise you use, ask students to think quickly and creatively. Be sure students have the paper before the exercise begins. A contest can be made out of these exercises by awarding a prize to the student who has the most creative ideas. Prizes could include extra credit points, a small trinket, or candy.

2. Tell students that these brainstorming exercises should be giving them practice in being creative. Ask students what creativity is and where it originates. Are some people more creative than others? Why? How does one remain creative? Tell students that creativity involves looking at the world in an unusual way.

3. Have composition buddies brainstorm the following situations.

   What would happen to the world if . . .

   - it got hotter every day?

   - everyone lost his or her sense of sight?

   Tell students to list their ideas without worrying about spelling or writing complete sentences—they should focus on being creative. To wrap up the exercise, ask students to share their ideas with the class.

4. Distribute **Handout 32** and let students brainstorm together as they complete the handout. They may choose to write more than one answer for each line. Share the best answers with the class.

5. Distribute **Handout 33**. Instruct students to choose one response from **Handout 32** and to write the statement in the middle of the wheel on **Handout 33**. Tell students that they will be writing a one-paragraph essay about the topic "If I were . . ."

6. Tell students to write six examples that support their topic on the inner spokes of the wheel on **Handout 33**. Then students should write on the outer spokes details that support the examples on the inner spokes. Collect, grade, and return **Handout 33**.

7. Distribute and review **Handout 34** before students begin writing. You may choose to add other qualifications to the chart. Tell students that when they complete the writing assignment, they should be sure they have met the requirements of each item on the chart, put a check mark in the student column, and stapled the charts to their essays. Explain that you will return the writing chart with the paper after it is graded, with checks in the teacher column for items that are correct.

8. Tell students to review their lists of transitional words, sensory adjectives, and onomatopoeia words. Direct them to complete a copy of the synonym chart (**Handout 19**), which they should have in their composition folders.

9. As students begin writing, remind them what the formula TS-6EX-SS means (Topic Sentence—Six Examples—Summary Sentence) and how to use it.

   • Use the words in the middle of the wheel to write a complete topic sentence.

   • Combine the words on each inner spoke with the details on its outer spoke to write six long, complete sentences.

   • Write a summary statement that contains an opinion or a comment about the future.

10. When students are finished with their paragraphs, tell them to complete the student column on **Handout 34**. Then they should staple **Handouts 19, 33,** and **34** to their paragraphs and turn everything in for a grade.

11. Distribute **Handout 35** and have students complete it.

12. Distribute **Handout 36**. Tell students to choose one feeling from **Handout 35** and use it to complete this statement: "Things that make me feel . . . ." Have students write the statement in the middle of the wheel on **Handout 36.**

13. Tell students to write the examples for their topic on the inner spokes of the wheel on **Handout 36**. Next, students should write details on the outer spokes that support the examples on the inner spokes. Collect, grade, and return **Handout 36.**

14. Distribute **Handout 37** before students begin writing. Review how students are to use this handout (see procedure 7).

15. Tell students to review their lists of transitional words, sensory adjectives, and onomatopoeia words. Direct them to complete a synonym chart (**Handout 19**), which they should have in their composition folders.

16. As students begin writing, remind them what the formula TS-6EX-SS means (Topic Sentence—Six Examples—Summary Sentence) and how to use it (see procedure 9).

17. When they are finished with their paragraphs, tell students to complete the student column on **Handout 37**. Then they should staple **Handouts 19, 36,** and **37** to their paragraphs and turn everything in for a grade.

18. Distribute **Handout 38** and have students complete it. Tell students to let their imaginations run wild. Share the best answers with the class. Remind students that creativity can improve any type of writing.

Name_____

Date_____

If I Were . . .

Directions: Complete the following. You may write more than one idea for each line.

1. If I were an animal, I'd be

2. If I were a TV show, I'd be

3. If I were a car, I'd be

4. If I were a city, I'd be

5. If I were a pet, I'd be

6. If I were a flower, I'd be

7. If I were a movie, I'd be

8. If I were a board game, I'd be

9. If I were a famous person, I'd be

10. If I were food, I'd be

11. If I were a piece of furniture, I'd be

12. If I were a sport, I'd be

© COPYRIGHT, The Center for Learning. Used with permission. Not for resale.

Formula Writing Basics
Lesson 7
Handout 33

Name_____

Date_____

"If I Were" Detailed Essay Wheel

Directions: Put your favorite statement from **Handout 32** in the middle of the wheel. Fill the inner spokes with six examples about the topic. Then fill the outer spokes with specific details about your examples.

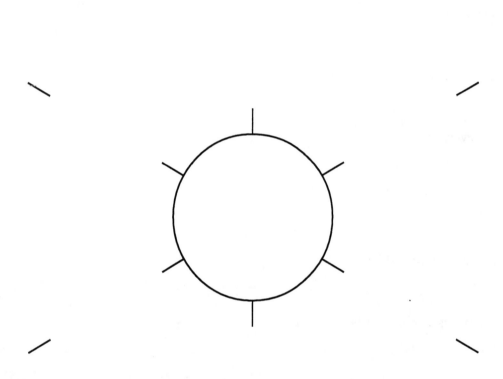

© COPYRIGHT, The Center for Learning. Used with permission. Not for resale.

Name_____

Date_____

"If I Were" Essay Writing Chart

Directions: Before you turn in your paper, review this checklist to be sure you have met all the requirements. When you are sure of each item, put a check mark under the student column. Staple this chart to your paper. Your teacher will put check marks in the teacher column for what is correct.

Writing Checklist	Student	Teacher
Student indented the paragraph.		
Student followed the formula TS-6EX-SS.		
Student used one transitional word.		
Student used one simile or metaphor.		
Student used two adjectives.		
Student used one onomatopoeia word.		
Student used synonyms.		
Student did not repeat the same noun, adjective, or verb more than three times.		
Student wrote complete sentences.		
Student used at least six to eight words in each sentence.		
Student capitalized the first letter of each sentence.		
Student used correct punctuation at the end of each sentence.		
Student checked spelling.		
Student reread the essay.		

© COPYRIGHT, The Center for Learning. Used with permission. Not for resale.

Feelings

Directions: Everyone has feelings. Sometimes we are happy and other times we are sad. We have moments when we are ashamed or afraid, brave or daring. Writing about our feelings is fun. Brainstorm six things that make you experience each feeling listed below.

1. happy

2. sad

3. angry

4. fearful

5. loving

6. hateful

© COPYRIGHT, The Center for Learning. Used with permission. Not for resale.

Name_____

Date_____

Feelings Detailed Essay Wheel

Directions: Choose one feeling from **Handout 35** and use it to complete the statement "Things that make me feel. . . ." Write the statement in the middle of the wheel. Fill the inner spokes with the six examples of your statement from **Handout 35.** Then fill the outer spokes with specific details about each example.

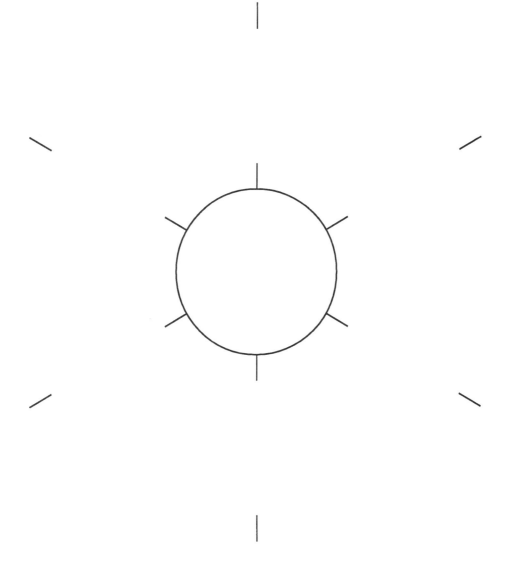

© COPYRIGHT, The Center for Learning. Used with permission. Not for resale.

Name_____

Date_____

Feelings Essay Writing Chart

Directions: Before you turn in your paper, review this checklist to be sure you have met all the requirements. When you are sure of each item, put a check mark under the student column. Staple this chart to your paper. Your teacher will put check marks in the teacher column for what is correct.

Writing Checklist	Student	Teacher
Student indented the paragraph.		
Student followed the formula TS-6EX-SS.		
Student used one transitional word.		
Student used one simile or metaphor.		
Student used two adjectives.		
Student used one onomatopoeia word.		
Student used synonyms.		
Student did not repeat the same noun, adjective, or verb more than three times.		
Student wrote complete sentences.		
Student used at least six to eight words in each sentence.		
Student capitalized the first letter of each sentence.		
Student used correct punctuation at the end of each sentence.		
Student checked spelling.		
Student reread the essay.		

© COPYRIGHT, The Center for Learning. Used with permission. Not for resale.

Name_____

Date_____

Be Creative!

Directions: Complete the following.

1. List five things that are soft.

2. List seven things that are blue.

3. Name three unusual uses for a shoelace.

4. Name three unusual uses for a button.

5. How would you improve a bookbag? a bike? a TV set?

6. What number are you? Why?

7. List ten things that are white.

8. List five things that are bumpy.

9. List six things above your neck that come in pairs.

10. What color is Monday? Wednesday? Friday? Sunday? Explain your choices.

© COPYRIGHT. The Center for Learning. Used with permission. Not for resale.

Lesson 8
Combining Sentences

Objective
- To write long sentences that express ideas clearly and directly

Notes to the Teacher

An important part of good writing is learning how to extend an idea. Even though you have asked students to write long, complete sentences in Lessons 1–7, students tend to write short, choppy sentences instead of combined sentences that flow smoothly. Once students learn the techniques introduced in this lesson, they will be able to write long, flowing sentences that show how ideas are related.

In this lesson, students learn to combine sentences using conjunctions and adjectives. They practice this skill in handout exercises and conclude the lesson by writing an essay that contains at least one long, complete sentence.

Procedure

1. Write the following on the board:

    Joseph is a handsome boy. He likes football.

    Joseph is a handsome boy, and he likes football.

    Ask students what the difference is between the two examples. As needed, point out that the first example includes two sentences while the second example is one sentence about the same topic. Explain that sentences, or independent clauses, can be combined by using the conjunctions *and, or,* or *but.*

2. Have students complete **Handout 39**. Review responses with the class.

3. Teach students that sentences can be lengthened by adding adjectives, transitional words, or groups of words. Demonstrate by writing the following on the board:

    Joseph is a handsome boy. He likes football.

    Joseph is a strong, handsome boy, and he likes to play a tough game of football.

4. Have students complete **Handout 40**. Tell students that each set of short sentences should be combined into one long sentence. Check their work for logical combinations.

5. Teach students that they can combine two sentences with *because.* Demonstrate by writing the following on the board:

    We will not go swimming. It is raining.

    We will not go swimming because it is raining.

6. Have students complete **Handout 41**. Direct students to share their answers with their composition buddies.

7. Extend the lesson by asking students to write paragraphs using the TS-6EX-SS formula and a long sentence. Assign one of the following topics. Simplify the topics or suggest different topics depending on the ability level of your students.

    - Describe a famous person you would like to be related to and why.

    - Describe your house or apartment.

    - Explain why you like or don't like Halloween.

8. Distribute **Handout 42** and remind students how to cluster.

    - Write the topic of the essay in the middle of the wheel.

    - Brainstorm six related ideas for the inner spokes.

    - On the outer spokes, write details that support the examples on the inner spokes.

    Collect, grade, and return **Handout 42** to students.

9. Distribute and review **Handout 43** before students begin writing. You may choose to add other qualifications to the chart. Tell students that when they complete the writing assignment, they should be sure they have met the requirements of each item on

the chart, put a check mark in the student column, and stapled the charts to their essays. Explain that you will return the writing chart with the paper after it is graded, with checks in the teacher column for items that are correct.

10. Tell students to review their lists of transitional words, sensory adjectives, and onomatopoeia words. Direct them to complete a synonym chart (**Handout 19**), which they should have in their composition folders.

11. As students begin writing, remind them what the formula TS-6EX-SS means (Topic Sentence—Six Examples—Summary Sentence) and how to use it.

- Use the words in the middle of the wheel to write a complete topic sentence.

- Combine the words on each inner spoke with the details on its outer spoke to write six long, complete sentences.

- Write a summary statement that contains an opinion or a comment about the future.

12. When they are finished with their paragraphs, tell students to complete the student column on **Handout 43**. Then they should staple **Handouts 19**, **42**, and **43** to their paragraphs and turn everything in for a grade.

Name_____

Date_____

Combining Sentences with Conjunctions

Directions: Use *and, but,* or *or* to join each pair of sentences. Make sure the new sentence makes sense.

1. This movie is interesting. I liked that one better.

2. Should allowances be given to children? Should they work for them?

3. It was an excellent party. We hope to go to the next one.

4. James delivered the mail on time. His customers liked his promptness.

5. The girls planned to attend the concert. They didn't get home in time.

6. He is a happy boy. People enjoy being with him.

7. A dark room is all right. I'm in the mood for a light color.

8. She likes this dress. That one looks better on her.

9. Do you want a cupcake? Would you rather have a cookie?

10. The new house is fireproof. It burned anyway.

© COPYRIGHT, The Center for Learning. Used with permission. Not for resale.

Name_____

Date_____

Combining Sentences

Directions: Combine the sentences grouped together into one long sentence.

The Hair

1. Robert looked in the mirror.
2. He combed his hair.
3. It was long.
4. It was wavy.

5. He combed the bangs.
6. He combed the sides.

7. The wind blew.
8. His hair moved.

9. Robert looked in the mirror again.
10. Robert combed his hair.

Mall Scene

1. A woman walked in the mall.
2. She stopped to look at a coat.

3. The coat was blue.
4. The coat was on sale.

5. She liked the coat.
6. She put the coat on.

© COPYRIGHT, The Center for Learning. Used with permission. Not for resale.

7. The coat was long.
8. The coat was warm.
9. The coat was soft.

10. She took the coat off.
11. She got in line.
12. She paid for the coat.

13. Now she has a big bag.
14. The bag is heavy.

Hamburgers

1. The patties are pink.
2. They are raw.

3. They are in the pan.
4. The pan is black.
5. They are ready to cook.

6. They begin to cook.
7. They smell good.
8. The patties are almost done.
9. The patties are smaller.

10. Put the patties on buns.
11. Put them on a plate.

© COPYRIGHT, The Center for Learning. Used with permission. Not for resale.

Name_____

Date_____

Combining Sentences with *Because*

Part A.

Directions: Make longer sentences by combining the two sentences with the word *because.*

1. We went downstream to fish. There were too many people upstream.

2. The rangers carried walkie-talkies. They wanted to keep in close contact.

3. Herb had a good time. He caught many fish.

4. The boys cooked breakfast beside the stream. There was clean water.

5. The forest is a frightening place. A storm could come up.

Part B.

Directions: Complete the sentences.

1. I like school because

2. My mother likes a quiet house because

3. The game was over because

4. You're expected to be more responsible because

5. One can't stay up late on a school night because

6. Children should eat their vegetables because

7. The classroom became quiet because

8. We went downstairs because

9. My parents want me to get good grades because

10. It is fun to play games because

© COPYRIGHT, The Center for Learning. Used with permission. Not for resale.

Name_____

Date_____

Combining Sentences Detailed Essay Wheel

Directions: Write the topic in the middle of the wheel. Fill the inner spokes with examples of the topic. Then fill the outer spokes with specific details about the examples on the inner spokes.

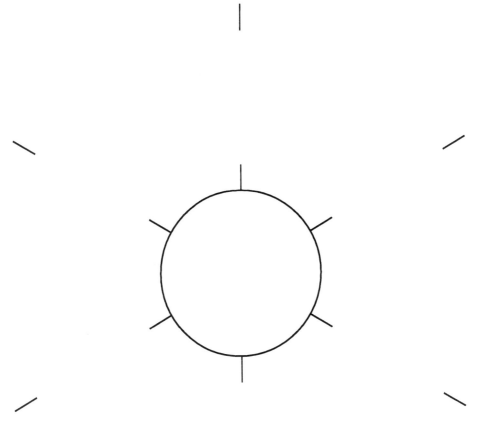

© COPYRIGHT. The Center for Learning. Used with permission. Not for resale.

Name_____

Date_____

Combining Sentences Essay Writing Chart

Directions: Before you turn in your paper, review this checklist to be sure you have met all the requirements. When you are sure of each item, put a check mark under the student column. Staple this chart to your paper. Your teacher will put check marks in the teacher column for what is correct.

Writing Checklist	Student	Teacher
Student indented the paragraph.		
Student followed the formula TS-6EX-SS.		
Student used one transitional word.		
Student used one simile or metaphor.		
Student used two adjectives.		
Student used one onomatopoeia word.		
Student used synonyms.		
Student did not repeat the same noun, adjective, or verb more than three times.		
Student wrote complete sentences.		
Student used at least six to eight words in a sentence.		
Student used the word *because* or another conjunction to write a long sentence.		
Student capitalized the first letter of each sentence.		
Student used correct punctuation at the end of each sentence.		
Student checked spelling.		
Student reread the essay.		

© COPYRIGHT, The Center for Learning. Used with permission. Not for resale.

Lesson 9
Grammar

Objective
- To write grammatically correct sentences

Notes to the Teacher
Students are learning to write essays that are structured, but they need to be grammatically correct within that structure. Now is a good time to tackle any persistent grammatical problems that your students have demonstrated during Lessons 1–8.

Make a list of the most common grammatical errors in students' writing. Using a grammar book's exercises for these problems is an effective tool for correcting students' grammatical mistakes. Giving students specific exercises related to the grammatical errors most prevalent in their writing is usually much more effective than teaching a unit of grammar in isolation.

Once you have taught a particular grammar rule, include it on writing charts for future writing assignments. For example, if you teach plurals, add a requirement for the correct usage of plurals. Including a grammar rule on a writing chart will reemphasize what you have taught and hold the students responsible for the material.

In this lesson, students correct various grammatical mistakes.

Procedure
1. Put two sentences that contain grammatical errors on the board daily. A good time for this exercise is when students enter the classroom at the beginning of the day or when they return from another activity. Write the number of errors each sentence contains in front of each sentence. Give the students a few minutes to write corrected sentences. Ask students for the correct answers so that the whole class will know the answers. Have students keep these papers in their composition folders. Work on specific problems each week and give students a small quiz at the end of each week to see if they have learned the material.

If you have trouble making up incorrect sentences each day, use examples from a grammar book. The following sentences demonstrate particular grammatical errors and may be used for daily exercises.

Proper nouns and period

(7) mr clark camped in ander state park

Mr. Clark camped in Ander State Park.

Verb, proper nouns, homonym, period

(4) jim has wore his knew shoes

Jim has worn his new shoes.

Commas in a series, proper nouns, period

(5) aunt wilma made cookies cakes and pies

Aunt Wilma made cookies, cakes, and pies.

Capitalization, verb, commas, quotation marks, period

(8) the children shaked the bottle and I said i think we are out of sauce

The children shook the bottle, and I said, "I think we are out of sauce."

Homonym, verb, capitalization, spelling, plurals, period

(5) their seems to be alot of problems

There seem to be a lot of problems.

Capitalization, proper noun, question mark

(4) will al let frank borrow the money

Will Al let Frank borrow the money?

Capitalization, title of magazine, period

(4) i put the latest issue of parents back on the shelf

I put the latest issue of Parents *back on the shelf.*

Pronoun order and case, capitalization, period

(4) me and bob went fishing

Bob and I went fishing.

Subject/verb agreement, capitalization, period

(3) kim don't think she is wrong

Kim doesn't think she is wrong.

2. Instead of giving weekly quizzes, give students a paragraph with many mistakes to correct. Such paragraphs can relate to other subjects (history, geography) being taught. Seeing the mistakes in an essay rather than in isolated sentences helps students learn to proofread.

3. Have students complete **Handout 44**. Review the finished exercise as a class.

Suggested Response:

The Day It Rained Cats and Dogs

> *One day the sky was gray, and it looked like rain. Sam and Bobby were going to their cousin's house to play. They wanted to play outside. When they arrived at Jim's house, they started to play basketball and were having fun. But it started to rain. The boys ran into the house and were sad. They heard loud noises on the house's roof and ran to the window to see what was going on outside. It was raining so hard they were scared. The cats and dogs in the neighborhood were making a loud fuss. They were howling and throwing themselves around. It sounded like it was raining cats and dogs.*

Name_____

Date_____

Grammatically Correct

Directions: Rewrite the following paragraph, correcting the mistakes.

The Day It Rained Cat's and Dogs

    one day the sky was gray and it looked like reign. Sam & Bobby where going to there cousins house to play. they wanted to play out side When they arrived at Jim's house they started to play basket ball and were having fun. But it started to rain. The boys' ran in to the house and were sad. They herd loud noises on the houses roof and ran too the window to see what was going on outside. it was raining so heard they were scared The cat's and dog's in the neighborhood where making a loud fuss. they were howling and throwing themselves around. it sounded like it was raining cat's and dog's.

© COPYRIGHT, The Center for Learning. Used with permission. Not for resale.

Lesson 10
Writing a Summary

Objective

- To write a summary paragraph following the formula TS-5EX-SS

Notes to the Teacher

Now that students can cluster their ideas and write simple essays, they may expand their prewriting skills to tackle more complex writing assignments. Students are introduced to a method that will help them analyze reading selections. Not only will the analysis method help their writing, but it will also carry over into other subjects and activities, including reading newspapers and watching television. Expect students to be motivated that their analysis and writing skills are advancing to the point that they may tackle writing summary paragraphs about short stories, book chapters, and videos.

In this lesson, students review several points they have learned about writing and are given a reading and writing assignment. They are introduced to the SQ3R method (Survey the Material, Question, Read the selection, Recite the answers, Review the selection), which they can use to analyze a reading selection. Students learn to complete an essay wheel based on information they gather from a reading selection. After the students have completed the wheel, they learn a step-by-step method of writing a summary, knowing at the end of the lesson what to do and what is expected of them.

Point out to students that the formula for this lesson is TS-5EX-SS (Topic Sentence—Five Examples—Summary Sentence).

Procedure

1. Write *SQ3R* on the board. Ask students what they think it is or what they think it means. After some discussion, tell students that SQ3R is a five-step method that will give them a more effective approach to studying written material. Using the method will help them gather information they need to write summary paragraphs about material they have read. SQ3R stands for Survey the material, Question, Read the selection, Recite the answers, and Review the selection.

2. Review the following definitions with students.

   Survey the material—look over an entire reading selection to get a general idea of what it is about. The reader should skim the selection, read its titles and headings, and note any illustrations.

   Question—mentally prepare a set of questions about the selection before reading it. Readers should keep in mind that they always need to look for answers to the questions *who, what, when, where,* and *why* as they read.

   Read the selection—read the material while looking for answers to the *who, what, when, where,* and *why* questions. When used as part of a writing assignment, answers to the questions will be used to fill the inner spokes of an essay wheel.

   Recite the answers—recite in your own words the answers to the *who, what, when, where,* and *why* questions.

   Review the selection—skim the reading or notes about the reading to memorize the main points of the selection.

3. Distribute **Handout 45**. Display the handout as a chart or transparency and review it with the class. Tell students to keep the handout in their composition folders.

4. Distribute **Handout 46** and assign a reading selection. Tell the students to complete the handout as they read. Instruct students to decide what the topic of the reading is and to write this topic in the center of the summary wheel. Next, fill the inner spokes of the wheel with examples from the reading that answer the questions *who, what, when, where* and *why.* On each outer spoke, students should write details that support the answer given on its inner spoke.

   Collect, grade, and return **Handout 46**.

5. Distribute and review **Handout 47** before students begin writing. You may choose to add other qualifications to the chart. Tell students that when they complete the writing assignment, they should be sure they have met the requirements of each item on the chart, put a check mark in the student column, and stapled the charts to their essays. Explain that you will return the writing chart with the paper after it is graded, with checks in the teacher column for items that are correct.

6. Tell students to review their lists of transitional words, sensory adjectives, and onomatopoeia words. Direct them to complete a synonym chart (**Handout 19**), which they should have in their composition folders.

7. As students begin writing, remind them what the formula TS-5EX-SS means (Topic Sentence—Five Examples—Summary Sentence) and how to use it. Remind students that for this writing assignment, they use five examples.

   • Use the words in the middle of the wheel to write a complete topic sentence.

   • Combine the words on each inner spoke with the details on its outer spoke to write five long, complete sentences.

   • Write a summary statement that contains an opinion or a comment about the future.

8. When they are finished with their paragraphs, tell students to complete the student column on **Handout 47**. Then they should staple **Handouts 19**, **46**, and **47** to their paragraphs and turn everything in for a grade.

Name_____

Date_____

The SQ3R Method

Directions: When you read, use the SQ3R method outlined below to help you understand the selection.

Using SQ3R

Survey the material

Look over what you will be reading. Check the titles, headings, and illustrations.

Question

Prepare to answer the questions *who, what, when, where,* and *why.*

Read the selection

Look for the answers to the questions.

Recite the answers

In your own words, recite the answers to the questions.

Review the selection

Quickly skim your notes and memorize the main points.

© COPYRIGHT, The Center for Learning. Used with permission. Not for resale.

Name_____

Date_____

A Detailed Summary Wheel

Directions: Follow the SQ3R method as you read your assigned selection. Write the topic of the passage in the center of the wheel. On the inner spokes, briefly answer the questions *who, what, when, where,* and *why.* On the outer spokes, add specific details about what you have written on the inner spokes.

© COPYRIGHT, The Center for Learning. Used with permission. Not for resale.

Name_____

Date_____

Summary Writing Chart

Directions: Before you turn in your essay, review this checklist to be sure you have met all the requirements. When you are sure of each item, put a check mark in the student column. Staple this chart to your paper. Your teacher will put check marks in the teacher column for what is correct.

Writing Checklist	Student	Teacher
Student indented the paragraph.		
Student followed the formula TS-5EX-SS.		
Student answered the questions *who, what, when, where,* and *why.*		
Student used one transitional word.		
Student used one simile or metaphor.		
Student used three adjectives.		
Student used one onomatopoeia word (optional).		
Student used synonyms.		
Student did not repeat the same noun, adjective, or verb more than three times.		
Student wrote complete sentences.		
Student used at least six to eight words in each sentence.		
Student used the word *because* or another conjunction to write a long sentence.		
Student capitalized the first letter of each sentence.		
Student used correct punctuation at the end of each sentence.		
Student checked spelling.		
Student reread the essay.		

© COPYRIGHT, The Center for Learning. Used with permission. Not for resale.

Lesson 11
A One-paragraph
Personal Narrative Essay

Objective
- To write a one-paragraph personal narrative essay following a formula

Notes to the Teacher
To write a good personal narrative, students must learn to be aware of sensory experiences. They also have to discover meaning in what has happened to them. Writing about these events gives their experiences significance.

Students can use the formula TS-6EX-SS (Topic Sentence—Six Examples—Summary Sentence) to write a personal narrative. Students learn to divide their stories into three parts: the beginning, the middle, and the end. The beginning reveals who, what, when, and where to set up the story. The middle section explains the event; the end brings the tale to an interesting close.

The narrative essay clusters introduced in this lesson are more complex than the wheels used in previous lessons. Students may need to spend more time learning how to use them.

In this lesson, students learn to write a personal narrative paragraph, first as part of a class exercise and then on their own. Students add **Handout 48**, a list of narrative transitional words, to their composition folders. Students also learn how to enrich their narrative essay with the adjectives, similes, metaphors, personification, and onomatopoeia introduced to them in earlier lessons.

Procedure
1. Write the following topics on the board.
   - My greatest hope
   - When I was helpful to someone
   - My happiest day
   - The day I met my best friend
   - The first day of school
   - My favorite summer

   As a class, pick one topic to be the subject of a narrative paragraph written during class. Tell the class that *narrative* is another word for story.

2. Distribute **Handout 48**, a list of transitional words that are helpful in narrative writing. Students should keep this list in their composition folders.

3. Distribute **Handout 49** and review it. You may choose to add other qualifications to the chart. Tell the class that when the writing assignment is complete, the class will check that it has met the requirements and will put a check mark in the class column.

4. Tell students to review their lists of transitional words, sensory adjectives, onomatopoeia words, and narrative transitional words.

   As a class, complete a copy of the synonym chart **(Handout 19)**, which students should have in their composition folders. Remind students that adding a simile or metaphor and using personification or onomatopoeia will make an essay more vivid.

5. Display a transparency of **Handout 50** and write the chosen topic on it, or draw the handout's clusters on the board and write the topic above them.

6. Explain that the beginning of a story sets up the *who, what, when,* and *where* of the story. The middle section describes the events. The ending brings the tale to an interesting close. Tell the class that the wheel marked *B* represents the story's beginning, the wheel marked *M* represents the story's middle, and the wheel marked *E* represents the story's end.

   As a class, fill the inner spokes of the wheels. For the *B* (beginning) wheel, use the four inner spokes to answer the *who, what, when,* and *where* questions about the story. Fill the inner spokes of the *M* (middle) wheel with information about what happens in the story. Fill the inner spokes of the *E* (end) wheel with examples of how the story comes to an interesting close.

7. When the inner spokes are filled, draw outer spokes for each inner spoke on the wheels (see **Handout 50**). Fill each outer spoke with details that support the information on the inner spoke. If the class decides that more spokes are needed to tell the story, add them.

8. Use the formula TS-6EX-SS to write the story. (If you have added spokes to the wheels, be sure to change the formula.)

   As a class, write a topic sentence for the story. Write this sentence and the rest of the paragraph on a different section of the board or on a new transparency.

   The next step is to write one long, complete sentence that combines the information on the inner and outer spokes for *who* and *what*. Then write one long, complete sentence that combines the information on the inner and outer spokes for *when* and *where*.

   As a class, write a long sentence for each pair of inner and outer spokes on wheels *M* and *E*. Finally, the class should write a summary sentence to end the story paragraph. Remind students that summary sentences either state an opinion or make a comment about the future.

9. Ask students to decide if the paragraph composed in class meets the requirements on the writing chart (**Handout 49**). Allow them to make the decision for each item on the chart. After students have completed the class column, review the chart with the class. Explain how you would fill out the teacher column. Discuss why you and the students believe the paragraph did or did not meet the requirements.

10. Tell students to pick their own topic for a personal narrative paragraph. If they have trouble doing so, you may suggest that they use a topic suggested in procedure 1 that was not the topic the class used.

11. Distribute **Handout 50**. Tell students to write their topic on the top of the page. Remind students that the beginning of a story sets up the *who, what, when,* and *where* of the story. The middle section tells what happened. The ending brings the event to an interesting close. Remind the class that wheel *B* represents the story's beginning, wheel *M* represents the story's middle, and wheel *E* represents the story's end.

12. Allow time for students to fill the inner spokes of the wheels. Remind them that the four inner spokes on wheel *B* answer the *who, what, when,* and *where* questions about the story. The inner spokes of wheel *M* should be filled with examples that tell what happens in the story. The inner spokes of wheel *E* should be filled with examples of how the story comes to an interesting close.

When the inner spokes are filled, tell students to fill each outer spoke with details that support the information on each inner spoke. Tell students to add more spokes as needed.

Collect, grade, and return **Handout 50**.

13. Distribute and review **Handout 51** before students begin writing. You may choose to add other qualifications to the chart. Tell students that when they complete the writing assignment, they should be sure they have met the requirements of each item on the chart, put a check mark in the student column, and stapled the charts to their essays. Explain that you will return the writing chart with the paper after it is graded, with checks in the teacher column for items that are correct.

14. Tell students to review their lists of transitional words, sensory adjectives, onomatopoeia words, and narrative transitional words. Direct them to complete a synonym chart (**Handout 19**), which they should have in their composition folders. Remind students to use figurative language or onomatopoeia to make their essays more vivid.

15. As students begin writing, remind them what the formula TS-6EX-SS means (Topic Sentence—Six Examples—Summary Sentence) and how to use it. (See procedure 8.) Remind students to change the formula if they added additional spokes.

16. When students have finished their paragraphs, tell them to complete the student column on **Handout 51**. Then they should staple **Handouts 19**, **50**, and **51** to their paragraphs and turn them in for a grade. Share the best paragraphs with the class.

Optional Activities

1. Cut out a picture from a magazine. Create a story about the picture and write a narrative paragraph to tell your story.

2. Choose one of the following topics to write another personal narrative paragraph.

   - I remember a day I was sad.
   - I remember shopping for school clothes.
   - I remember my favorite birthday.
   - I remember a time I was proud.
   - I remember a good time.
   - I remember a bad time.

Name_____

Date_____

Narrative Transitional Words

Directions: Use this list each time you write a narrative essay. Keep this paper in your folder and add any useful words or phrases as you learn them.

first

then

soon

next

eventually

after

presently

second

finally

later

at the beginning

in the middle

afterward

by the time

© COPYRIGHT, The Center for Learning. Used with permission. Not for resale.

Name_____

Date_____

Personal Narrative Essay Writing Chart 1

Directions: As a class, review this checklist to be sure you have met all the requirements. When you are sure of each item, put a check mark in the class column. Your teacher will tell you what items would be checked as correct in the teacher column.

Writing Checklist	Class	Teacher
Class indented the paragraph.		
Class followed the formula TS-6EX-SS.		
Class filled the wheels completely.		
Class answered the questions *who, what, when,* and *where.*		
Class used one transitional word.		
Class used one simile or metaphor.		
Class used three adjectives.		
Class used one onomatopoeia word.		
Class used synonyms.		
Class did not repeat the same noun, adjective, or verb more than three times.		
Class wrote complete sentences.		
Class used at least six to eight words in each sentence.		
Class used the word *because* or another conjunction to write a long sentence.		
Class capitalized the first letter of each sentence.		
Class used correct punctuation at the end of each sentence.		
Class checked spelling.		
Class reread the essay.		

© COPYRIGHT, The Center for Learning. Used with permission. Not for resale.

Name_____

Date_____

A Personal Narrative Essay Wheel

Directions: Write your topic on this page. Use the inner spokes of wheel *B* to answer the *who, what, when,* and *where* questions about the story. Fill the inner spokes of wheel *M* with what happened. The inner spokes of wheel *E* should bring the story to an interesting close. After you fill the inner spokes, complete the outer spokes with specific details about each inner spoke.

Topic _____

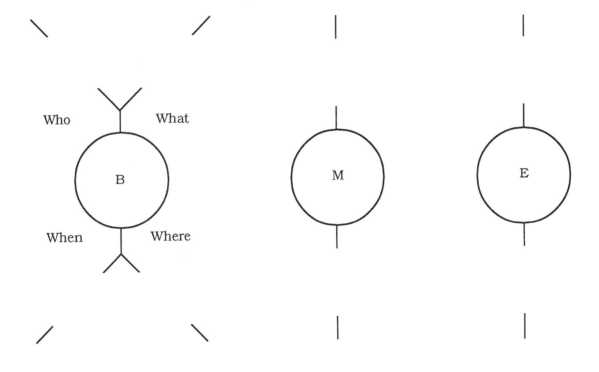

© COPYRIGHT, The Center for Learning. Used with permission. Not for resale.

Name_____

Date_____

Personal Narrative Essay Writing Chart 2

Directions: Before you turn in your essay, review this checklist to be sure you have met all the requirements. When you are sure of each item, put a check mark in the student column. Staple this chart to your paper. Your teacher will put check marks in the teacher column for what is correct.

Writing Checklist	Student	Teacher
Student indented the paragraph.		
Student followed the formula TS-6EX-SS.		
Student filled the wheels completely.		
Student answered the questions *who*, *what*, *when*, and *where*.		
Student used one transitional word.		
Student used one simile or metaphor.		
Student used three adjectives.		
Student used one onomatopoeia word.		
Student used synonyms.		
Student did not repeat the same noun, adjective, or verb more than three times.		
Student wrote complete sentences.		
Student used at least six to eight words in each sentence.		
Student used the word *because* or another conjunction to write a long sentence.		
Student capitalized the first letter of each sentence.		
Student used the correct punctuation at the end of each sentence.		
Student checked spelling.		
Student reread the essay.		

© COPYRIGHT, The Center for Learning. Used with permission. Not for resale.

Lesson 12
A One-paragraph Fictional Narrative Essay

Objective
- To write a one-paragraph fictional narrative essay using a formula

Notes to the Teacher
The purpose of the fictional narrative essay is to write a new story using details from an article that the students have read. The students will follow the same formula TS-6EX-SS (Topic Sentence—Six Examples—Summary Sentence) as the personal narrative essay from Lesson 11, but will base the fictional narrative paragraph on fact and imagination—facts used from material read and the imagination of the writer.

Gathering information for a fictional narrative paragraph is not difficult. It simply consists of recalling and developing all the details needed to create a new story. The writer must be careful not to stray too far from the main story line or include details that interrupt the flow of the narrative. The writer should also attempt to make the story as interesting as possible by choosing sharp, precise words and incorporating imagery to develop the ideas. Close attention to choosing the right words will help the resulting story, a combination of information and creation, to be vivid and effective.

In this lesson, students use the SQ3R method (Survey the material, Question, Read the selection, Recite the answers, Review the selection) to help them gather information from a reading selection. They cluster and complete a writing chart as they write a fictional narrative essay. Their essay is a creative story that uses information from the reading.

Procedure
1. Read the article on **Handout 52** to the class. Tell students that they will use the facts in the reading to create their own stories about a cat and his hunting adventure.

2. Review the SQ3R method with students. Tell students that SQ3R is a five-step method that provides an effective approach to studying written material. SQ3R stands for Survey the material, Question, Read the selection, Recite the answers, and Review the selection. Using the method will help students gather information they need to write summary paragraphs about material they have read.

3. Display **Handout 45** as a chart or transparency and review it with the class. If you have already taught Lesson 10, students should have this handout in their composition folders.

Review the following definitions with students.

Survey the material—look over an entire reading selection to get a general idea of what it is about. The reader should skim the selection, read its titles and headings, and note any illustrations.

Question—mentally prepare a set of questions about the selection before reading it. Readers should keep in mind that they always need to look for answers to the questions *who, what, when, where,* and *why* as they read.

Read the selection—read the material while looking for answers to the *who, what, when, where,* and *why* questions. When used as part of a writing assignment, answers to the questions will be used to fill the inner spokes of an essay wheel.

Recite the answers—recite in your own words the answers to the *who, what, when, where,* and *why* questions.

Review the selection—skim the reading or notes about the reading to memorize the main points of the selection.

4. Distribute **Handout 52** and have students use the SQ3R method to complete it.

5. Distribute **Handout 53** and have students write the topic of the story being created at the top of the page. Make students aware of the following points.

   - The beginning of a story sets up the *who, what, when,* and *where* of the story.

   - The middle section of a story tells about what happens.

   - The end section of a story brings the event to an interesting close.

   - The wheel marked *B* represents the story's beginning.

   - The wheel marked *M* represents the story's middle.

   - The wheel marked *E* represents the story's end.

6. Have students fill the inner spokes of the wheels with examples from the story they are creating. Remind students that the four inner spokes on wheel *B* answer the *who, what, when,* and *where* questions about the story. Tell students to fill the inner spokes of wheel *M* with examples that tell what happens in the fictional story. Then students should fill the inner spokes of wheel *E* with examples of how the story comes to an interesting close.

   When the inner spokes are filled, tell students to fill each outer spoke with facts that support the information on its inner spoke. *The outer spokes should be facts that were found in the article on* **Handout 52***.* Students can add more spokes as needed.

   Collect, grade, and return **Handout 53** to students.

7. Distribute and review **Handout 54** before students begin writing. You may choose to add other qualifications to the chart. Tell students that when they complete the writing assignment, they should be sure they have met the requirements of each item on the chart, put a check mark in the student column, and stapled the charts to their essays. Explain that you will return the writ-

ing chart with the paper after it is graded, with checks in the teacher column for the items that are correct.

8. Tell students to review their lists of transitional words, sensory adjectives, onomatopoeia words, and narrative transitional words. Direct them also to complete a copy of the synonym chart (**Handout 19**), which they should have in their composition folders.

9. As students begin writing, remind them what the formula TS-6EX-SS means (Topic Sentence—Six Examples—Summary Sentence) and how to use it.

   - Use the words at the top of the handout to write a topic sentence.

   - Write a long, complete sentence that combines the information on the inner and outer spokes for *who* and *what* (wheel *B*).

   - Write a long complete sentence that combines the information on the inner and outer spokes of *when* and *where* (wheel *B*).

   - Write long, complete sentences for each pair of inner and outer spokes on wheels *M* and *E*.

   - Write a summary sentence that states an opinion or makes a comment about the future.

   Remind students to change the formula if they added additional spokes.

9. When students have finished their paragraphs, tell them to complete the student column on **Handout 54**. Then they should staple **Handouts 19, 53,** and **54** to their paragraphs and turn everything in for a grade. Share the best paragraphs with the class.

Optional Activity

1. Read an article of your choice. Write a one-paragraph fictional narrative essay based on your reading.

Name_____

Date_____

The Unpredictable Cat

Directions: Read the article using the SQ3R method. Underline the parts that you wish to use as details for your new story.

If you have a cat, you know how unpredictable such an animal can be. Cats can roll on their back and ask you to pet them or ignore you completely. Sometimes they can be charming and other times they can turn into hunters. In fact, cats have a double identity. They have been companions to human beings for a long time, but they have never forgotten the ways of their wild ancestors.

All cats belong to the *Felidae* family, which is divided into three main groups. The first group is made up of the big, wild cats—lions, tigers, leopards, and jaguars. The second group consists only of cheetahs. The third group includes small wild cats, such as the bobcat, lynx, and leopard cat, and also includes all the domestic or tame cats.

The members of the cat family share many of the same characteristics and habits. All cats eat mainly meat. Cats that live in the wild must hunt and kill other animals to get their food. Keen hearing and vision help them locate animals in the forest. Long, flexible bodies and padded feet allow them to crouch low to the ground and sneak up on their prey. Powerful, muscled legs make cats fast-moving; sharp teeth make them swift killers.

Though most tame cats are fed by their owners, some still kill mice or birds. Cats can't change their urge to hunt any more than they can change their whiskers or their tails.

© COPYRIGHT, The Center for Learning. Used with permission. Not for resale.

Fictional Narrative Essay Wheels

Directions: Write your topic at the top of the page. Fill the inner spokes of the wheels with examples from your new story's beginning, middle, and end. The inner spokes of wheel *B* should answer the *who, what, when,* and *where* questions about the story. The inner spokes of wheel *M* should tell what happened. The inner spokes of wheel *E* should bring the story to an interesting close. After you fill the inner spokes, complete the outer spokes with facts that were found in "The Unpredictable Cat" on **Handout 52**.

Topic _____

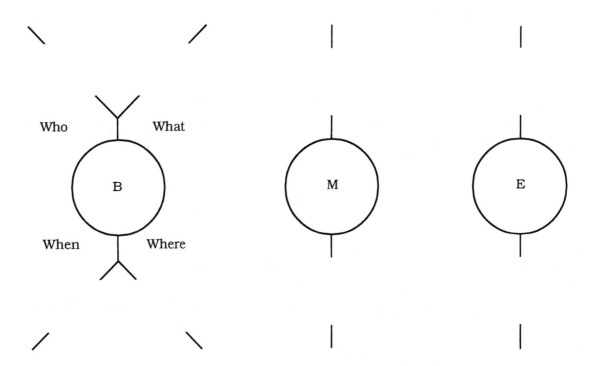

© COPYRIGHT, The Center for Learning. Used with permission. Not for resale.

Name_____

Date_____

A Fictional Narrative Essay Writing Chart

Directions: Before you turn in your essay, review this checklist to be sure you have met all the requirements. When you are sure of each item, put a check mark in the student column. Staple this chart to your paper. Your teacher will put check marks in the teacher column for what is correct.

Writing Checklist	Student	Teacher
Student indented the paragraph.		
Student followed the formula TS-6EX-SS.		
Student filled the wheels completely.		
Student answered the questions *who, what, when,* and *where.*		
Student used facts from the article on the outer spokes of the wheels.		
Student used one transitional word.		
Student used one simile or metaphor.		
Student used three adjectives.		
Student used one onomatopoeia word.		
Student used synonyms.		
Student did not repeat the same noun, adjective, or verb more than three times.		
Student wrote complete sentences.		
Student used at least six to eight words in each sentence.		
Student used the word *because* or another conjunction to write a long sentence.		
Student capitalized the first letter of each sentence.		
Student used correct punctuation at the end of each sentence.		
Student checked spelling.		
Student reread the essay.		

© COPYRIGHT, The Center for Learning. Used with permission. Not for resale.

Lesson 13
Friendly Letters

Objective
- To write a friendly letter using a formula

Notes to the Teacher

Writing friendly letters is a common, everyday task for most students. Yet it requires special skills and knowledge that are important to understand. For example, friendly letters (and invitations) have a definite form: date, greeting, body, and closing. Friendly letters and invitations should be easy for students to write once they learn to use the formula Date + Greeting + Body + Closing and the Body formula, TS-6EX-SS (Topic Sentence—Six Examples—Summary Sentence). Correct comma placement is also discussed. If needed, refer to a grammar book for appropriate exercises.

In this lesson, students write two friendly letters, one of which is a narrative friendly letter. For each letter, students cluster and complete a writing chart.

Procedure

1. Put the following topics on the board and have the students select one.

   - Explain why your team lost the game.

   - Explain why students like your school.

   - Describe your family.

   Explain that all the topics call for an expository or descriptive paragraph. Tell the students that they are going to write a letter to a friend about the topic they chose.

2. Distribute **Handout 55**. This handout shows the correct form of a friendly letter and gives the two formulas that the students should memorize. The first formula is Date + Greeting + Body + Closing. Have students review **Handout 55** while you explain that the first part of the formula is the date at the top on the right side of the paper. The second item is the greeting. This simply addresses the person to whom the student is writing. Next is the body, a paragraph describing the message of the letter. Explain that the closing includes a phrase, such as *yours truly* or *sincerely yours*, and the writer's name.

The second formula is TS-6EX-SS (Topic Sentence—Six Examples—Summary Sentence). The number of examples you assign could be less, according to the ability level of the students. This formula should be used for the body portion of the letter.

Read the letter on **Handout 55** aloud. Point out that students should place commas between the day and year, after the greeting, and after the closing. Provide students with exercises in correct comma placement in letters if students need to practice this skill.

3. Distribute **Handout 56** and remind students how to cluster.

   - Write the topic of the essay in the middle of the wheel.

   - Brainstorm six related ideas for the inner spokes.

   - On the outer spokes, write details that support the examples on the inner spokes.

   Collect, grade, and return **Handout 56** to students.

4. Distribute and review **Handout 57** before students begin writing. You may choose to add other qualifications to the chart. Tell students that when they complete their letters, they should be sure they have met the requirements of each item on the chart, put a check mark in the student column, and stapled the charts to their essays. Explain that you will return the writing chart with the paper after it is graded, with checks in the teacher column for items that are correct.

5. Tell students to review their lists of transitional words, sensory adjectives, onomatopoeia words, and **Handout 55**. Direct them to complete a synonym chart (**Handout 19**), which they should have in their composition folders.

6. As students begin writing, remind them what the two formulas (Date + Greeting + Body + Closing and TS-6EX-SS) mean and how to use them. If necessary, refer to procedure 2 and the following steps.

- Use the words in the middle of the wheel to write a complete topic sentence.

- Combine the words on each inner spoke with the details on its outer spoke to write six long, complete sentences.

- Write a summary statement that contains an opinion or a comment about the future.

7. When students are finished with their letters, tell them to complete the student column on **Handout 57**. Then they should staple **Handouts 19**, **56**, and **57** to the letter and turn everything in for a grade.

8. Tell students that a friendly letter can also be a narrative letter. Put the following topics on the board and have the students select one.

- Tell about a time when you won an award.

- Tell about a time when you did something nice.

- Tell about a time when you were surprised.

Explain that all the topics call for a narrative paragraph. Tell the students they are going to write a narrative letter to a friend about the topic they chose.

9. Distribute **Handout 58**, narrative friendly letter writing wheels. Have students write the topic they have chosen at the top of the page. Make students aware of the following points.

- The beginning of a narrative sets up the who, what, when, and where of the story.

- The middle section tells about what happens.

- The end section brings the event to an interesting close.

- The wheel marked *B* represents the story's beginning.

- The wheel marked *M* represents the story's middle.

- The wheel marked *E* represents the story's end.

10. Have students fill the inner spokes of the wheels. Remind students that for wheel *B*, they fill the four inner spokes with answers to the *who, what, when,* and *where* questions about the story. Have students fill the inner spokes of wheel *M* with examples that tell what happens in the story. Then students should fill the inner spokes of wheel *E* with examples of how the story comes to an interesting close. When the inner spokes are filled, tell the students to fill each outer spoke with details that support the information on its inner spoke. Students can add more spokes as needed.

Collect, grade, and return **Handout 58** to students.

11. Distribute and review **Handout 59** before students begin writing. You may choose to add other qualifications to the chart. Tell students that when they complete the letter, they should be sure they have met the requirements of each item on the chart, put a check mark in the student column, and stapled the charts to their letters. Explain that you will return the writing chart with the letter after it is graded, with checks in the teacher column for the items that are correct.

12. Tell students to review their lists of transitional words, sensory adjectives, onomatopoeia words, narrative transitional words, and **Handout 55**. Tell them to complete a copy of the synonym chart (**Handout 19**), which they should have in their composition folders. Remind students to use figurative language or onomatopoeia to make their letters more vivid.

13. As students begin writing, remind them what the formulas (Date + Greeting + Body + Closing and TS-6EX-SS) mean and how to use them. If necessary refer to procedure 2 and the following steps.

- Use the words at the top of the handout to write a topic sentence.

- Write a long, complete sentence that combines the information on the inner and outer spokes for *who* and *what* (wheel *B*).

- Write a long, complete sentence that combines the information on the inner and outer spokes of *when* and *where* (wheel *B*).

- Write long, complete sentences for each pair of inner and outer spokes on wheels *M* and *E*.

- Write a summary sentence that states an opinion or makes a comment about the future.

14. When students have finished their letters, tell them to complete the student column on **Handout 59**. Then they should staple **Handouts 19**, **58**, and **59** to the letter and turn everything in for a grade.

Optional Activity

1. Select one of the following topics and write a friendly letter.

   - Tell your fairy godmother all the wishes you would like to have come true.

   - Tell a friend who has moved away everything that is happening at school and in the neighborhood.

   - Tell a grandparent what has been happening in your city.

   - Tell a brother or sister away at college how things at home are different when he or she is away.

Name_____

Date_____

Friendly Letters: Correct Form

Directions: A friendly letter is a letter you might write to a friend, relative, or acquaintance. The sample letter below shows the correct form for this type of letter. Notice that the body paragraph uses the formula TS-6EX-SS (Topic Sentence—Six Examples—Summary Sentence).

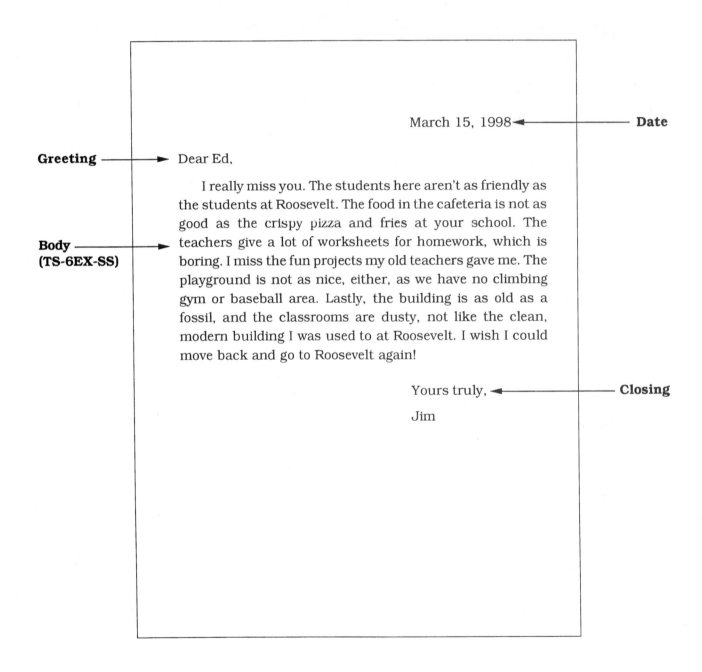

Greeting

Body (TS-6EX-SS)

March 15, 1998 — **Date**

Dear Ed,

I really miss you. The students here aren't as friendly as the students at Roosevelt. The food in the cafeteria is not as good as the crispy pizza and fries at your school. The teachers give a lot of worksheets for homework, which is boring. I miss the fun projects my old teachers gave me. The playground is not as nice, either, as we have no climbing gym or baseball area. Lastly, the building is as old as a fossil, and the classrooms are dusty, not like the clean, modern building I was used to at Roosevelt. I wish I could move back and go to Roosevelt again!

Yours truly, — **Closing**

Jim

© COPYRIGHT, The Center for Learning. Used with permission. Not for resale.

Name_____

Date_____

Friendly Letter Wheel

Directions: Write the topic of your choice in the center of the wheel. Fill the inner spokes with six examples about your topic. Then fill the outer spokes with specific details about the examples.

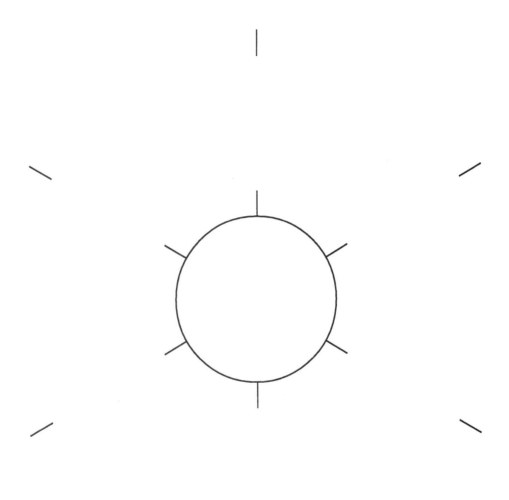

© COPYRIGHT, The Center for Learning. Used with permission. Not for resale.

Name_____

Date_____

Friendly Letter Writing Chart

Directions: Before you turn in your essay, review this checklist to be sure you have met all the requirements. When you are sure of each item, put a check mark in the student column. Staple this chart to your paper. Your teacher will put check marks in the teacher column for what is correct.

Writing Checklist	Student	Teacher
Student indented the paragraph.		
Student followed the formula Date + Greeting + Body + Closing.		
Student followed the formula TS-6EX-SS in the body paragraph.		
Student used commas correctly.		
Student used one transitional word.		
Student used one simile or metaphor.		
Student used three adjectives.		
Student used one onomatopoeia word.		
Student used synonyms.		
Student did not repeat the same noun, adjective, or verb more than three times.		
Student wrote complete sentences.		
Student used at least six to eight words in each sentence.		
Student used the word *because* or another conjunction to write a long sentence.		
Student capitalized the first letter of each sentence.		
Student used correct punctuation at the end of each sentence.		
Student checked spelling.		
Student reread the essay.		

© COPYRIGHT, The Center for Learning. Used with permission. Not for resale.

Name_____

Date_____

Narrative Friendly Letter Wheels

Directions: Write your topic at the top of the page. Use the inner spokes of wheel *B* to answer the *who, what, when,* and *where* questions about the story. Fill the inner spokes of wheel *M* with what happened. The inner spokes of wheel *E* should bring the story to an interesting close. After you fill the inner spokes, complete the outer spokes with specific details about each inner spoke.

Topic _____

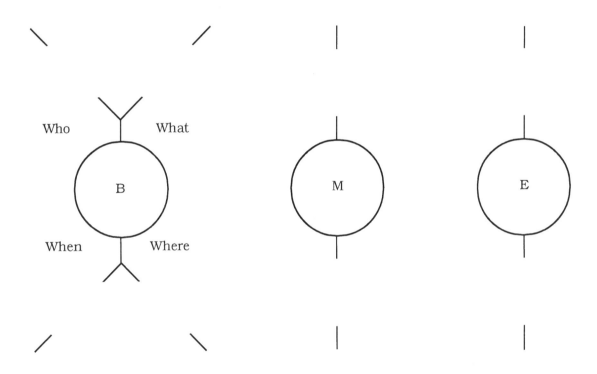

© COPYRIGHT, The Center for Learning. Used with permission. Not for resale.

Name_____

Date_____

Narrative Friendly Letter Writing Chart

Directions: Before you turn in your letter, review this checklist to be sure you have met all the requirements. When you are sure of each item, put a check mark in the student column. Staple this chart to your letter. Your teacher will return this checklist with the items checked that are correct.

Writing Checklist	Student	Teacher
Student indented the paragraph.		
Student followed the formula Date + Greeting + Body + Closing.		
Student followed the formula TS-6EX-SS in the body paragraph.		
Student filled the wheels completely.		
Student answered the questions *who, what, when,* and *where* in the body paragraph.		
Student used commas correctly.		
Student used one transitional word.		
Student used one simile or metaphor.		
Student used three adjectives.		
Student used one onomatopoeia word.		
Student used synonyms.		
Student did not repeat the same noun, adjective, or verb more than three times.		
Student wrote complete sentences.		
Student used at least six to eight words in each sentence.		
Student used the word *because* or another conjunction to write a long sentence.		
Student capitalized the first letter of each sentence.		
Student used correct punctuation at the end of each sentence.		
Student checked spelling.		
Student reread the essay.		

© COPYRIGHT, The Center for Learning. Used with permission. Not for resale.

Lesson 14
Journal Writing

Objective
- To write a journal entry using a formula

Notes to the Teacher
People have kept journals and diaries for centuries. Journal writing is an excellent way for students to record interesting ideas, thoughts, feelings, impressions, and experiences. Student journals can become treasure chests of writing ideas. Decide if you want students to purchase an additional notebook to use as a journal.

Because journals will be introduced to students as a risk-free writing assignment, you may choose to use writing charts for journal entries but not grade the entries. You may wish to make journal writing assignments periodically. Or, you may wish to give extra credit to students who write journal entries that are not assigned in class.

In this lesson, students learn expectations for journal writing and write narrative, expository, and descriptive journal entries. Students are also provided with topics for beginning a journal.

Procedure
1. Ask students what goes into a journal or diary. You may want to read aloud a short excerpt from a diary to pique students' interest, especially if such an excerpt supports another subject you are teaching, such as history.

2. Distribute **Handout 60** and discuss its content. Note that people have been keeping journals and diaries for centuries and that journals are important to writers. Explain that most entries require five to ten minutes of writing and cover about two-thirds of a page. Tell students to make a habit of carrying their journals with them so that they can jot down ideas during the day. Ask students to keep **Handout 60** in their composition folders.

3. To get students' journals started, distribute **Handout 61**. Make a transparency of the handout or draw its cluster on the board. Write the words *simple pleasures* in the middle of the wheel and ask students to do the same on **Handout 61**. Give an example of a simple pleasure in your life and write it on one of the inner spokes. Ask students to write some of the simple pleasures in their lives on the inner spokes on their wheels. Then tell students to write details on the outer spokes that support what they have written on the inner spokes.

Collect, grade, and return **Handout 61**.

4. Distribute and review **Handout 62** before students begin writing. You may choose to add other qualifications to the chart, such as requiring students to title their journal entries. Tell students that when they complete their journal entries, they should be sure they have met the requirements of each item on the chart, put a check mark in the student column, and attached the charts to their journals. Explain that you will return the writing charts with the journals, with checks in the teacher column for items that are correct.

5. Tell students to review their lists of transitional words, sensory adjectives, and onomatopoeia words, and **Handout 60**. Direct them to complete a copy of the synonym chart (**Handout 19**), which they should have in their composition folders.

6. As students begin writing, remind them what the formula TS-6EX-SS means (Topic Sentence—Six Examples—Summary Sentence) and how to use it.
   - Use the words in the middle of the wheel to write a complete topic sentence.
   - Combine the words on each inner spoke with the details on its outer spoke to write six long, complete sentences.
   - Write a summary statement that contains an opinion or a comment about the future.

7. When they are finished with their journal entries, tell students to complete the student column on **Handout 62**. Then they should attach **Handouts 19**, **61**, and **62** to their journals and turn them in.

8. Tell students that now they will write a narrative journal entry. If they have trouble choosing a topic, suggest that they write a narrative entry about a favorite day.

9. Distribute **Handout 63** and tell students to write the topic of the narrative journal entry at the top of the page. Make students aware of the following points.

   - The beginning of a story sets up the *who, what, when,* and *where* of the story.

   - The middle section of a story tells what happened.

   - The end section of a story brings the event to an interesting close.

   - The wheel marked *B* represents the story's beginning.

   - The wheel marked *M* represents the story's middle.

   - The wheel marked *E* represents the story's end.

   Have students fill the inner spokes of the wheels. Remind students that for wheel *B*, they now have four inner spokes to fill to answer the *who, what, when,* and *where* questions about the narrative. Tell students to fill the inner spokes of wheel *M* with examples that tell what happens in the narrative. Then students should fill the inner spokes of wheel *E* with examples of how the narrative comes to an interesting close.

   When the inner spokes are filled, tell students to fill each outer spoke with details that support the information on each inner spoke. Students can add more spokes as needed.

   Collect, grade, and return **Handout 63**.

10. Distribute and review **Handout 64** before students begin writing. (See procedure 4).

11. Tell students to review their lists of transitional words, sensory adjectives, onomatopoeia words, narrative transitional words, and **Handout 60**. Direct them to complete a copy of the synonym chart (**Handout 19**), which they should have in their composition folders. Remind students to use figurative language or onomatopoeia to make their entries more vivid.

12. As students begin to write, remind them what the formula TS-6EX-SS means (Topic Sentence—Six Examples—Summary Sentence) and how to use it.

    - Use the words at the top of the handout to write a topic sentence.

    - Write a long, complete sentence that combines the information on the inner and outer spokes for *who* and *what* (wheel *B*).

    - Write a long, complete sentence that combines the information on the inner and outer spokes of *when* and *where* (wheel *B*).

    - Write long, complete sentences for each pair of inner and outer spokes on wheels *M* and *E*.

    - Write a summary sentence that states an opinion or makes a comment about the future.

13. When students have finished their narrative journal entries, tell them to complete the student column on **Handout 64**. Then they should attach **Handouts 19**, **63**, and **64** to their journals and turn them in.

14. Distribute **Handout 65** and encourage students to add their own ideas to this list of possible journal entries. Students should keep this handout in their composition folders so they can refer to it for journal writing ideas.

Name_____

Date_____

Expectations for Journal Writing

Directions: Read the following information. Keep this page in your composition folder.

1. Journal entries may be observations, memories, dreams, questions, letters, stories, descriptions, conversations, or ideas.

2. Journals are a place to write honest thoughts.

3. Journals are a place to experiment with language and explore ideas. Journals provide writing practice.

4. Journals are a place to make observations.

5. Journals help writers discover writing topics.

6. Journal entries should be dated. Over a period of time, writers see their ideas develop and change, and they begin to understand themselves better.

7. Writers may share their entries with others but are never forced to do so. Journals are read only by the teacher, who may comment on the writing.

© COPYRIGHT. The Center for Learning. Used with permission. Not for resale.

Name_____

Date_____

Journal Entry Wheel

Directions: Write your topic in the middle of the wheel. Fill the inner spokes with six examples about the topic. Then fill the outer spokes with specific details about your examples.

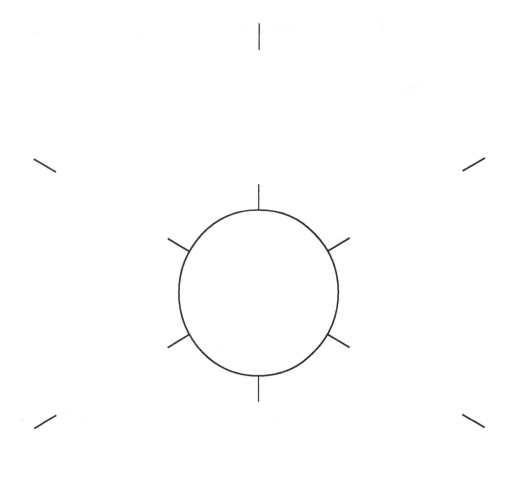

© COPYRIGHT, The Center for Learning. Used with permission. Not for resale.

Name_____

Date_____

Journal Entry Writing Chart

Directions: Before you turn in your journal entry, review this checklist to be sure you have met all the requirements. When you are sure of each item, put a check mark in the student column. Attach this chart to your journal. Your teacher will return this checklist with the items checked that are correct.

Writing Checklist	Student	Teacher
Student indented the paragraph.		
Student followed the formula TS-6EX-SS.		
Student dated the entry.		
Student used one transitional word.		
Student used one simile or metaphor.		
Student used three adjectives.		
Student used one onomatopoeia word.		
Student used synonyms.		
Student did not repeat the same noun, adjective, or verb more than three times.		
Student wrote complete sentences.		
Student used at least six to eight words in each sentence.		
Student used the word *because* or another conjunction to write a long sentence.		
Student capitalized the first letter of each sentence.		
Student used correct punctuation at the end of each sentence.		
Student checked spelling.		
Student reread the essay.		

© COPYRIGHT, The Center for Learning. Used with permission. Not for resale.

Name_____

Date_____

Narrative Journal Entry Wheels

Directions: Write your topic at the top of the page. Use the inner spokes of wheel *B* to answer the *who*, *what*, *when*, and *where* questions about the topic. Fill the inner spokes of wheel *M* with what happened. The inner spokes of wheel *E* should bring the entry to an interesting close. After you fill the inner spokes, complete the outer spokes with specific details about each inner spoke.

Topic _____

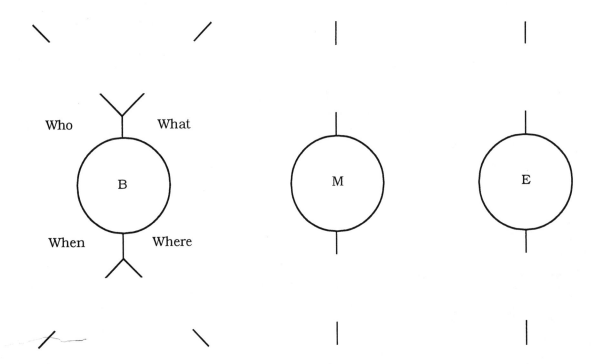

© COPYRIGHT, The Center for Learning. Used with permission. Not for resale.

Formula Writing Basics
Lesson 14
Handout 64

Name_____

Date_____

Narrative Journal Entry Writing Chart

Directions: Before you turn in your journal entry, review this checklist to be sure you have met all the requirements. When you are sure of each item, put a check mark in the student column. Attach this chart to your journal. Your teacher will return this checklist with the items checked that are correct.

Writing Checklist	Student	Teacher
Student indented the paragraph.		
Student followed the formula TS-6EX-SS.		
Student dated the entry.		
Student filled the wheels completely.		
Student answered the questions *who, what, when,* and *where.*		
Student used one transitional word.		
Student used one simile or metaphor.		
Student used three adjectives.		
Student used one onomatopoeia word.		
Student used synonyms.		
Student did not repeat the same noun, adjective, or verb more than three times.		
Student wrote complete sentences.		
Student used at least six to eight words in each sentence.		
Student used the word *because* or another conjunction to write a long sentence.		
Student capitalized the first letter of each sentence.		
Student used correct punctuation at the end of each sentence.		
Student checked spelling.		
Student reread the essay.		

© COPYRIGHT, The Center for Learning. Used with permission. Not for resale.

Name_____

Date_____

Topics for a Journal Entry

Directions: Your journal can be whatever you wish it to be. It is a place to practice writing and find writing topics. Entries may be observations, memories, dreams, questions, letters, stories, descriptions, conversations, or ideas.

Topic Suggestions

1. Describe yourself as a family member would describe you.

2. What are the three best things about you?

3. Describe a relative.

4. What are some things that make you interesting?

5. Describe a dream.

6. Write about an argument you had with someone.

7. Write a series of entries beginning with "I remember."

8. Tell about a time when you were helpful.

9. Describe an embarrassing moment.

10. Tell about a time when you were proud.

11. Write about summer vacation.

12. Tell about your favorite holiday.

13. Tell about a time you were sad.

14. Describe a friend.

15. Describe your favorite game.

© COPYRIGHT, The Center for Learning. Used with permission. Not for resale.

Lesson 15
Writing Directions

Objective
- To write directions using a formula

Notes to the Teacher
Writing directions is not easy. Students will learn that they need to be clear and logical to write good directions. By breaking up a process into step-by-step details, students can accurately explain how to accomplish a task. Writing directions is complicated for young students and can be practiced by having students read each others' essays aloud while other students follow the directions. Such an activity reinforces good listening skills, as the students following the directions must listen carefully.

In this lesson, students use the formula TS-6EX-SS (Topic Sentence—Six Examples—Summary Sentence) and a writing chart to write directions. They complete clusters and two writing assignments. Student-written directions are then demonstrated in class. Ingredients for a peanut-butter-and-jelly sandwich are needed during some demonstrations.

Procedure
1. Ask students how to make a bed. Depending on students' ability level, choose a simpler topic, such as how to sharpen a pencil. List students' comments on the board or on an overhead transparency.

2. Display a transparency of **Handout 66** or draw the cluster on the board. Add or delete spokes to match students' abilities. Point out that the spokes are numbered and explain that directions need to be organized and ordered from a first step to a last step.

3. Write the topic in the middle of the wheel. Ask students to name the first step for making a bed. Write their response on the first inner spoke. Complete the rest of the inner spokes in a similar fashion. Completed inner spokes should resemble the following:

   1. Throw off the top sheet, blanket, and bedspread.
   2. Smooth the bottom sheet.
   3. Fluff the pillow.

   4. Pull the top sheet and blanket up toward the pillow.
   5. Fold the top of the top sheet over the blanket.
   6. Pull up the bedspread to cover the pillow, blanket, and sheets.

4. Add an outer spoke to each inner spoke. Ask the class to help you write specific details about each inner spoke on the outer spokes. Completed outer spokes should be similar to the following:

   1. Shake out the top sheet, blanket, and bedspread.
   2. Push out the wrinkles.
   3. Place pillow at the head of the bed.
   4. Smooth the top sheet and blanket with your hands.
   5. Smooth out wrinkles.
   6. Add your favorite toy animals.

5. Discuss any problems the class may have had during the clustering process. Explain that every detail is needed and that someone writing directions should not be tempted to overlook a detail that doesn't seem important.

6. Ask students to think of a topic about which they can write directions. This topic must be something that can be done in the classroom, such as putting books on a shelf or drawing something on the chalkboard. Students should not tell anyone else what topic they have chosen. Check students' topics to determine that they can be done in the classroom.

7. Distribute **Handout 66** and tell students that they will write directions for another student to follow later.

   Have students write their topic in the middle of the wheel. Then they should write six steps that need to be followed to complete the task. These should be written in order on the numbered inner spokes. The outer spokes should be filled with specific details about the steps on the inner spokes.

   Collect, grade, and return **Handout 66**.

8. Distribute and review **Handout 67** before students begin writing. You may choose to add other qualifications to the chart. Tell students that when they complete the writing assignment, they should be sure they have met the requirements of each item on the chart, put a check mark in the student column, and stapled the charts to their paragraphs. Explain that you will return the writing chart with the paper after it is graded, with checks in the teacher column for the items that are correct.

9. Tell students to review their lists of transitional words, sensory adjectives, and onomatopoeia words. Direct them to complete a copy of the synonym chart (**Handout 19**), which they should have in their composition folders.

10. As students begin writing, remind them what the formula TS-6EX-SS means (Topic Sentence—Six Examples—Summary Sentence) and how to use it.

   • Use the words in the middle of the wheel to write a complete topic sentence.

   • Combine the words on each inner spoke with the details on its outer spoke to write six long, complete sentences.

   • Write a summary statement that contains an opinion or a comment about the future.

11. When students are finished with their paragraphs, tell them to complete the student column on **Handout 67**. Then they should staple **Handouts 19**, **66**, and **67** to their paragraphs and turn everything in for a grade.

12. Before you return the graded paragraphs to the students, choose one of the paragraphs for a class demonstration of how to write directions. The writer of the selected paragraph should read the directions while a volunteer listens carefully and follows the directions. As a class, discuss what happens. Ask students:

   • Do the directions make sense?

   • Is the student who was chosen to follow directions a good listener?

   • Can he or she follow directions?

If the directions didn't make sense, review the student writer's cluster. As a class, discuss how the steps on the wheel could have been clearer. As time permits, choose other paragraphs and repeat the exercise to demonstrate the difficulty of writing clear directions. Thank the students whose paragraphs were chosen for being good sports.

13. Distribute **Handout 68**, telling students that this will be their next topic for a writing assignment. Distribute **Handout 69** and tell students that they will write directions for another student to follow later.

14. Instruct students to write the topic, how to make a peanut-butter-and-jelly sandwich, in the middle of the wheel. Then they should write six steps that need to be followed to complete the task. These should be written in order on the numbered inner spokes. The outer spokes should be filled with specific details about the steps written on the inner spokes.

Collect, grade, and return **Handout 69**.

15. Distribute and review **Handout 70** before students begin writing (see procedure 8).

16. Tell students to review their lists of transitional words, sensory adjectives, and onomatopoeia words. Direct them to complete a synonym chart (**Handout 19**) which they should have in their composition folders.

17. As students begin writing, remind them what the formula TS-6EX-SS means (Topic Sentence—Six Examples—Summary Sentence) and how to use it (see procedure 10).

18. When students are finished with their paragraphs, tell them to complete the student column on **Handout 70**. Then they should staple **Handouts 19**, **69**, and **70** to their paragraphs and turn everything in for a grade.

19. Bring peanut butter, jelly, a plastic knife, and bread if these items are permitted in the classroom.

Before you return graded paragraphs to students, choose one of the paragraphs for a class demonstration of sandwich making. The writer of the selected paragraph should read the paragraph aloud while the other student listens carefully and follows the directions exactly.

As a class, discuss what happens. Ask students:

- Do the directions make sense?
- Is the student who was chosen to follow directions a good listener?
- Can he or she follow directions?

If the directions didn't make sense, review the writer's cluster. As a class, discuss how the steps on the wheel could have been clearer. As time permits, choose other paragraphs and repeat the exercise to demonstrate the difficulty of writing clear directions. Thank the students whose paragraphs were chosen for being good sports.

Name_____

Date_____

Directions Detailed Essay Wheel

Directions: Write your topic in the center of the wheel. On inner spoke 1, write the first step needed to complete the task. Complete the other inner spokes with the rest of the steps in order. On the outer spokes, write details about the steps on the inner spokes.

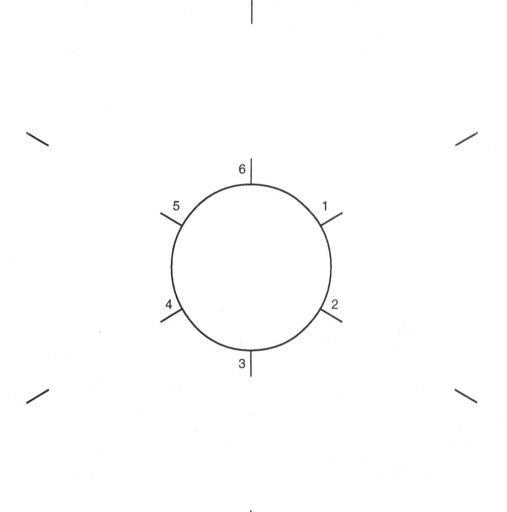

© COPYRIGHT, The Center for Learning. Used with permission. Not for resale.

Name_____

Date_____

Directions Writing Chart

Directions: Before you turn in your essay, review this checklist to be sure you have met all the requirements. When you are sure of each item, put a check mark in the student column. Staple this chart to your pages. Your teacher will return this checklist with the items checked that are correct.

Writing Checklist	Student	Teacher
Student indented the paragraph.		
Student followed the formula TS-6EX-SS.		
Student filled the wheel completely.		
Student used the numbered wheel spokes correctly.		
Student used two transitional words.		
Student used three adjectives.		
Student used synonyms.		
Student did not repeat the same noun, adjective, or verb more than three times.		
Student wrote complete sentences.		
Student used at least six to eight words in each sentence.		
Student used the word *because* or another conjunction to write a long sentence.		
Student capitalized the first letter of each sentence.		
Student used correct punctuation at the end of each sentence.		
Student checked spelling.		
Student reread essay.		

© COPYRIGHT, The Center for Learning. Used with permission. Not for resale.

Name_____

Date_____

A Sticky Situation

Directions: Look at the picture below, which shows what you need to make a delicious peanut-butter-and-jelly sandwich. Keep these items in mind when you receive your next writing assignment.

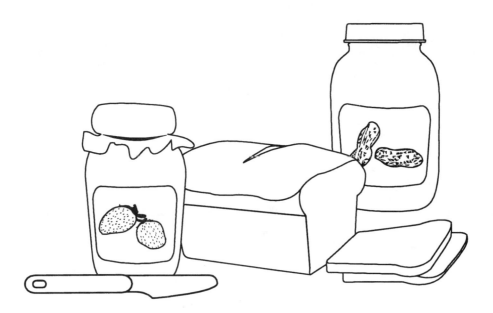

© COPYRIGHT, The Center for Learning. Used with permission. Not for resale.

Name_____

Date_____

Peanut-Butter-and-Jelly Sandwich Directions Wheel

Directions: Write your topic in the center of the wheel. On inner spoke 1, write the first step needed to complete the task. Complete the other inner spokes with the rest of the steps in order. On the outer spokes, write details about the steps on the inner spokes.

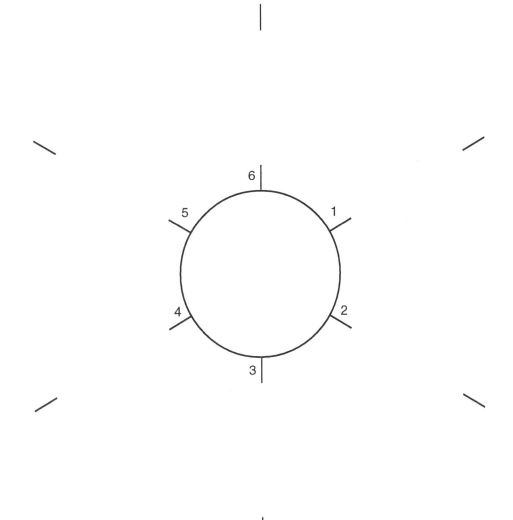

© COPYRIGHT, The Center for Learning. Used with permission. Not for resale.

Name_____

Date_____

Peanut-Butter-and-Jelly Sandwich Directions Writing Chart

Directions: Before you turn in your essay, review this checklist to be sure you have met all the requirements. When you are sure of each item, put a check mark in the student column. Staple this chart to your paper. Your teacher will return this checklist with the items checked that are correct.

Writing Checklist	Student	Teacher
Student indented the paragraph.		
Student followed the formula TS-6EX-SS.		
Student filled the wheel completely.		
Student used the numbered wheel spokes correctly.		
Student used two transitional words.		
Student used three adjectives.		
Student used synonyms.		
Student did not repeat the same noun, adjective, or verb more than three times.		
Student wrote complete sentences.		
Student used at least six to eight words in each sentence.		
Student used the word *because* or another conjunction to write a long sentence.		
Student capitalized the first letter of each sentence.		
Student used correct punctuation at the end of each sentence.		
Student checked spelling.		
Student reread the essay.		

© COPYRIGHT, The Center for Learning. Used with permission. Not for resale.

Lesson 16
Book Reports

Objective
- To write a book report using a formula

Notes to the Teacher
Book reports are a wonderful way to introduce reading and writing together. Such reports give students a chance to think and write about their independent reading assignments. In a fiction book report, students examine characterization. Writing biography book reports can provide students with needed role models.

In this lesson, students read fiction and biography books, learn how to take notes while they read, and write book reports. Students need to select books to read before the lesson begins. During the lesson, they need sufficient time out of class to read.

Procedure
1. Take students to the library and instruct them to sign out a fiction book.

2. Ask students how they find out what a character in a book they are reading is like. Ask them what an author does to show this. After some discussion, define *characterization* as the way a writer uses words to tell a story and to let the reader "get inside" the characters in the novel. By getting inside a character, the reader can see what a character is feeling, thinking, or becoming. The author shows the exterior of a character—his or her words, actions, and appearance—in such a way as to reveal the character's personality and emotional well-being.

3. Distribute **Handout 71** for students to complete as they read their fiction books. Explain that the more students write on the handout, the easier it will be for them to write their book report essays. After the students have read their novels and completed **Handout 71**, ask them to choose one of the following topics for their one-paragraph book report.

   - Describe the main character.
   - Describe the actions that make the main character unforgettable.
   - Discuss the qualities that set the main character apart from other characters.

Point out to students that all of these topics relate to characterization.

4. Distribute **Handout 72** for students to complete. Review the clustering process as needed.

   - Write the topic of the essay in the middle of the wheel.
   - Brainstorm six related ideas for the inner spokes.
   - On the outer spokes, write details that support the examples on the inner spokes.

   Tell students to refer to **Handout 71** for ideas to write on the wheel spokes.

   Collect, grade, and return **Handout 72.**

5. Distribute and review **Handout 73** before students begin writing. You may choose to add other qualifications to the chart. Direct students to title their book reports with the title of the book they read. When students complete their book reports, they should be sure they have met the requirements of each item on the chart, put a check mark in the student column, and stapled the charts to their essays. Explain that you will return the writing chart with the paper after it is graded, with checks in the teacher column for items that are correct.

6. Tell students to review their lists of transitional words, sensory adjectives, and onomatopoeia words. Direct them to complete a synonym chart **(Handout 19)**, which they should have in their composition folders.

7. As students begin writing, remind them what the formula TS-6EX-SS means (Topic Sentence—Six Examples—Summary Sentence) and how to use it.

   - Use the words in the middle of the wheel to write a complete topic sentence.
   - Combine the words on each inner spoke with the details on its outer spoke to write six long, complete sentences.
   - Write a summary statement that contains an opinion or a comment about the future.

8. When students are finished with their paragraphs, tell them to complete the student column on **Handout 73**. Then they should staple **Handouts 19**, **71**, **72**, and **73** to their paragraphs and turn everything in for a grade.

9. Take students to the library and instruct them to sign out a biography of a famous person.

10. Distribute **Handout 74** for students to complete as they read their books. Explain that the more students write on the worksheet, the easier it will be for them to write their book report essays. After the students have read their biographies and completed **Handout 74**, ask them to choose one of the following topics for their one-paragraph book report.

    • Why is this person famous?

    • What qualities does this person exhibit?

    • Who or what influenced this person?

    • What lessons can we learn from this person?

11. Distribute **Handout 75** for students to complete. Review how students are to use this handout. (See procedure 4.) Tell students to refer to **Handout 74** for ideas to write on the wheel spokes.

    Collect, grade, and return **Handout 75**.

12. Distribute **Handout 76** before students begin writing. Review how students are to use this handout. (See procedure 5.)

13. Tell students to review their lists of transitional words, sensory adjectives, and onomatopoeia words. Direct them to complete a synonym chart (**Handout 19**), which they should have in their composition folders.

14. Direct students to begin writing their essays. Review the steps as needed. (See procedure 7.)

15. When students are finished with their paragraphs, tell them to complete the student column on **Handout 76**. Then they should staple **Handouts 19**, **74**, **75**, and **76** to their paragraphs and turn everything in for a grade.

Optional Activities

1. Make an illustrated book cover for one of the book reports in this lesson.

2. Prepare a display of biographies and essays about the men and women most admired by your classmates.

Name_____

Date_____

Character Sketch Worksheet

Directions: Complete the following as you read your book.

Title of the book_____

Author_____

Name of the main character_____

1. Describe the physical appearance of the main character (color of hair and eyes, height, clothes, distinguishing features).

2. Describe the actions of the main character (silly, smart, brave).

3. List three qualities of the main character. Provide supporting examples.

4. List people who influence the main character.

5. List three things the main character likes to do.

6. How does the main character speak? Does he or she use slang or dialect?

7. What do other characters think of the main character? Is he or she liked or disliked?

8. What lessons can we learn from the main character?

© COPYRIGHT, The Center for Learning. Used with permission. Not for resale.

Formula Writing Basics
Lesson 16
Handout 72

Name_____

Date_____

Fiction Book Report Wheel

Directions: Write the topic in the center of the wheel. Fill the inner spokes with six examples that support the topic. Then fill the outer spokes with specific details that support your examples.

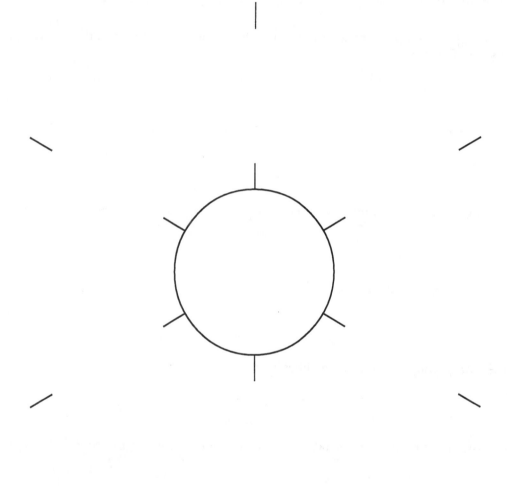

© COPYRIGHT, The Center for Learning. Used with permission. Not for resale.

Fiction Book Report Writing Chart

Directions: Before you turn in your essay, review this checklist to be sure you have met all the requirements. When you are sure of each item, put a check mark in the student column. Staple this chart to your paper. Your teacher will return this checklist with the items checked that are correct.

Writing Checklist	Student	Teacher
Student indented the paragraph.		
Student followed the formula TS-6EX-SS.		
Student completed **Handout 71**.		
Student used a title.		
Student used two transitional words.		
Student used one simile or metaphor.		
Student used three adjectives.		
Student used one onomatopoeia word.		
Student used synonyms.		
Student did not repeat the same noun, adjective, or verb more than three times.		
Student wrote complete sentences.		
Student used at least six to eight words in each sentence.		
Student used the word *because* or another conjunction to write a long sentence.		
Student capitalized the first letter of each sentence.		
Student used correct punctuation at the end of each sentence.		
Student checked spelling.		
Student reread the essay.		

© COPYRIGHT, The Center for Learning. Used with permission. Not for resale.

Biographical Sketch Worksheet

Directions: Complete the following as you read your book.

Title of the book_____

Author_____

Name of the subject of the biography _____

1. Describe the physical appearance of the subject (color of hair and eyes, height, clothes, distinguishing features).

2. Describe the actions of the subject (silly, smart, brave).

3. List three qualities of the subject. Provide supporting examples.

4. List people who influence the subject.

5. List three things the subject likes to do.

6. How does the subject speak? Does he or she use slang or dialect?

7. What do other characters think of the subject? Is he or she liked or disliked?

8. What lessons can we learn from the subject?

© COPYRIGHT, The Center for Learning. Used with permission. Not for resale.

Name_____

Date_____

Biography Book Report Wheel

Directions: Write the topic in the center of the wheel. Fill the inner spokes with six examples about the topic. Then fill the outer spokes with specific details about your examples.

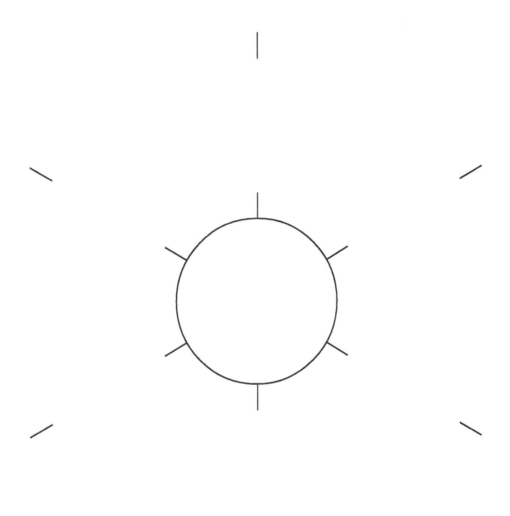

© COPYRIGHT, The Center for Learning. Used with permission. Not for resale.

Name_____

Date_____

Biographical Book Report Writing Chart

Directions: Before you turn in your essay, review this checklist to be sure you have met all the requirements. When you are sure of each item, put a check mark in the student column. Staple this chart to your paper. Your teacher will return this checklist with the items checked that are correct.

Writing Checklist	Student	Teacher
Student indented the paragraph.		
Student followed the formula TS-6EX-SS.		
Student completed **Handout 74**.		
Student used a title.		
Student used two transitional words.		
Student used one simile or metaphor.		
Student used three adjectives.		
Student used one onomatopoeia word.		
Student used synonyms.		
Student did not repeat the same noun, adjective, or verb more than three times.		
Student wrote complete sentences.		
Student used at least six to eight words in each sentence.		
Student used the word *because* or another conjunction to write a long sentence.		
Student capitalized the first letter of each sentence.		
Student used correct punctuation at the end of each sentence.		
Student checked spelling.		
Student reread the essay.		

© COPYRIGHT, The Center for Learning. Used with permission. Not for resale.

Lesson 17
Interviews

Objectives
- To learn interviewing skills
- To write an essay based on an interview

Notes to the Teacher
Learning to interview is an important skill. By knowing the right questions to ask, students can learn a great deal about a person interviewed and the subjects discussed. Students can also use their interviewing skills after they have read a book to interview an imaginary character or they can interview a person for a speech they are preparing. By following a format, students can plan ahead to make good use of time during an interview. By following a formula, students can write excellent interview essays.

In this lesson, students learn some basic interview guidelines. They interview another student, cluster, complete a writing chart, and write an essay based on the interview.

Procedure
1. Instruct students to choose someone in the class whom they do not know well. Tell the students that they will be interviewing that student on the next class day.

2. Write the following guidelines on the board or an overhead transparency and discuss them with the class.

   1. Write out three questions before an interview. Make sure the questions are broad.

   2. Never ask questions that can be answered *yes* or *no*. Ask questions that begin with *what, why,* or *how.*

   3. Take notes during the interview. Try to get four examples or facts in response to each question.

   4. Before you end the interview, check each direct quotation by reading it back to the interviewee at the end of the interview.

3. Because direct quotations help personalize and add color to the essays, review the following basic rules for quotation marks. Write sample sentences for each rule on the board or an overhead transparency.

   1. Use quotation marks at the beginning and end of a direct quotation.

      Bob said, "It is a great day to go swimming."

   2. A period at the end of a sentence goes inside the quotation marks.

      The girl said, "Let's go for a ride."

   3. A quoted statement at the beginning of a sentence is followed by a comma, which belongs inside the quotation marks.

      "Brush your teeth," said the dentist.

   4. If a quotation is divided by explanatory words, each part of the quotation is enclosed by quotation marks.

      "One very healthy exercise," said Melissa, "is skiing."

4. Distribute **Handout 77** and allow time for students to prepare questions.

5. Provide class time for interviews. Have students complete **Handout 77** as they conduct their interviews.

6. Distribute **Handout 78** and tell students that they will write a one-paragraph essay based on the interview.

7. Instruct students to write the name of the interviewee in the space provided. Point out that the wheel is divided into three sections. Each number refers to the questions asked during the interview. Tell students to write two examples that answer the first interview question on the inner spokes for section one. Students should complete the inner spokes for sections two and three in the same way. Finally, students should fill the outer spokes with details that support the examples on the inner spokes. Tell students to refer to **Handout 77** for material to write on the spokes. Tell students that they need to include a direct quotation on at least two spokes.

Collect, grade, and return **Handout 78.**

8. Distribute and review **Handout 79** before students begin writing. You may choose to add other qualifications to the chart. Tell students that when they complete their essays, they should be sure they have met the requirements of each item on the chart, put a check mark in the student column, and stapled the charts to their essays. Explain that you will return the writing chart with the paper after it is graded, with checks in the teacher column for items that are correct.

9. Tell students to review their lists of transitional words, sensory adjectives, and onomatopoeia words. Direct them to complete a synonym chart (**Handout 19**), which they should have in their composition folders.

10. As students begin writing, remind them what the formula TS-6EX-SS means (Topic Sentence—Six Examples—Summary Sentence) and how to use it.

    • Use the words in the middle of the wheel to write a complete topic sentence.

    • Combine the words on each inner spoke with the details on its outer spoke to write six long, complete sentences.

    • Write a summary statement that contains an opinion or a comment about the future.

11. When students are finished with their paragraphs, tell them to complete the student column on **Handout 79.** Then they should staple **Handouts 19**, **77**, **78**, and **79** to their paragraphs and turn everything in for a grade.

Optional Activities
1. Conduct an imaginary interview with a character in a novel and write an essay based on that interview. Add specific quotations from the novel to your essay.

2. Interview a family member and write an essay about that person.

Name_____

Date_____

Interview Sheet

Directions: Write three questions to ask during the interview. Try to ask questions beginning with *what*, *why*, and *how*. Avoid questions that can be answered *yes* or *no*. Use this page to record the responses. You need two direct quotations to include in your essay.

1.

2.

3.

© COPYRIGHT, The Center for Learning. Used with permission. Not for resale.

Name_____

Date_____

Interview Wheel

Directions: Write the name of the person you are interviewing in the space provided. Write two examples that answer the first interview question on the inner spokes for section 1. Then write two examples that answer the second interview question on the inner spokes for section 2. Write two examples that answer the third interview question on the inner spokes for section 3. On the outer spokes, write specific details about the examples on the inner spokes.

Name of person interviewed _____

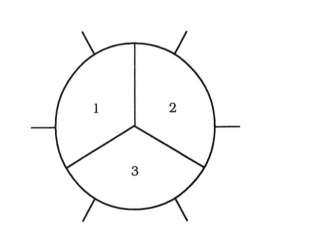

© COPYRIGHT, The Center for Learning. Used with permission. Not for resale.

Name_____

Date_____

Interview Writing Chart

Directions: Before you turn in your essay, review this checklist to be sure you have met all the requirements. When you are sure of each item, put a check mark in the student column. Staple this chart to your paper. Your teacher will return this checklist with the items checked that are correct.

Writing Checklist	Student	Teacher
Student indented the paragraph.		
Student followed the formula TS-6EX-SS.		
Student filled the wheel completely.		
Student answered each question on two wheel spokes.		
Student used two direct quotations.		
Student used two transitional words.		
Student used one simile or metaphor.		
Student used three adjectives.		
Student used one onomatopoeia word.		
Student used synonyms.		
Student did not repeat the same noun, adjective, or verb more than three times.		
Student wrote complete sentences.		
Student used at least six to eight words in each sentence.		
Student used the word *because* or another conjunction to write a long sentence.		
Student capitalized the first letter of each sentence.		
Student used correct punctuation at the end of each sentence.		
Student used quotation marks correctly.		
Student checked spelling.		
Student reread the essay.		

© COPYRIGHT, The Center for Learning. Used with permission. Not for resale.

Lesson 18
A Research Essay

Objectives
- To learn the elements of research
- To write a research essay using a formula

Notes to the Teacher
Research skills are needed to find facts and opinions on specific subjects. Students learn to find and interpret information through the elements of research: narrowing a topic, finding resource material, and taking notes. Students also write a short research essay by following the formula TS-6EX-SS (Topic Sentence—Six Examples—Summary Sentence). Knowing how to research and how to express research in writing are important skills that students can use their entire lives.

This lesson involves several skills often difficult for elementary students. If the material is too advanced for your students, this lesson can be omitted. However, the lesson may be simplified to suit students' abilities by

- not requiring students to use index cards for notes
- allowing students to record facts directly on **Handout 82**
- not requiring a written bibliography
- requiring students to use only one source
- decreasing the number of examples in the writing formula

To maximize the effort put into teaching research skills, use the research essay assignment to reinforce a topic being studied in science or social studies.

In this lesson, students research topics, take notes, write bibliography entries, and write a one-paragraph research essay. Index cards are needed for note taking.

Procedure
1. Ask students if they know what the phrase *to narrow a topic* means. After listening to students' responses, explain that when a writing topic is broadly stated, it often needs to be narrowed before one writes. As an example, tell students that a broad topic might be *plants* and ask how this topic might be narrowed. Guide the discussion as needed, suggesting that one way to narrow the topic would be to choose trees as a type of plant, pine trees as a type of tree, etc.

2. Distribute **Handout 80** and briefly discuss the topics listed. Tell students to choose first and second choice topics and narrow them. Students may choose other topics with your approval.

3. Explain to students that a *bibliography* is an alphabetized list of sources a writer used to write a research essay or article. The bibliography is placed at the end of the paper. Tell students that they will be writing a bibliography that includes three sources they used to write their research essays. Distribute **Handout 81** and review the sample entries. Ask students to keep the handout in their composition folders.

4. Take the students to the library to conduct a quick search for information. Choose students' sources based on their ability level. Have students use **Handout 81** to draft a working bibliography of at least three different sources. Explain to students that their bibliographies will grow as they read about their subjects.

   If students cannot find information or do not like their first choice topics, they may use their second choice topic to compile a working bibliography.

5. Once students have at least three entries, instruct them to record the bibliographic information for the first entry on an index card. Students should write a number 1 in the bottom right corner of the index card. Have students complete and number index cards for each entry on their working bibliographies. Tell students that they have just created their bibliographic cards.

6. Direct students to continue their research by using index cards to record the information they find. Tell them to write one idea on each card, using their own words, and to include the page number where they found the information. Students should write on the bottom right corner of this card the number of the bibliographic card for the source of the information. The cards they have just

created are research cards. Writing one idea on each index card allows for easy organization of ideas.

If students find new sources, they should add the source to their working bibliographies, create and number a bibliographic card for the source, and use this number on any research cards that use information from the source.

7. Tell students that they should complete at least twelve research cards (a minimum of four research cards from each of three sources of information).

8. When students are done gathering information, instruct them to write a final bibliography. Tell them to arrange their sources in alphabetical order according to the author's last name or the source's title. Ask students to use **Handout 81** as a guide.

9. Have students write their names on the backs of their bibliographic and research cards. Collect the cards and bibliographies to check that students have included enough sources and information. Return the cards and bibliographies to the students.

10. Distribute **Handout 82** and tell students that they will write a one-paragraph essay about their research topic.

Review the clustering process as needed.
- Write the topic of the essay in the middle of the wheel.
- Brainstorm six related ideas for the inner spokes.
- On the outer spokes, write details that support the examples on the inner spokes.

Students should refer to their research cards for information.

Collect, grade, and return **Handout 82**.

11. Distribute and review **Handout 83** before students begin writing. You may choose to add other qualifications to the chart. Tell students that when they complete their essays, they should be sure they have met the requirements of each item on the chart, put a check mark in the student column, and stapled the charts to their essays. Explain that you will return the writing chart with the paper after it is graded, with checks in the teacher column for items that are correct.

12. Tell students to review their lists of transitional words, sensory adjectives, and onomatopoeia words. Direct them to complete a synonym chart (**Handout 19**), which they should have in their composition folders.

13. As students begin writing, remind them what the formula TS-6EX-SS means (Topic Sentence—Six Examples—Summary Sentence) and how to use it.

- Use the words in the middle of the wheel to write a complete topic sentence.
- Combine the words on each inner spoke with the details on its outer spoke to write six long, complete sentences.
- Write a summary statement that contains an opinion or a comment about the future.

Tell students to title their essays with their topic.

14. When students are finished with their paragraphs, tell them to complete the student column on **Handout 83**. Then they should staple **Handouts 19**, **82**, and **83**, the essay, the bibliography, and the bibliographic and research cards together and turn everything in for a grade.

Optional Activity
1. Write a research essay using one of the speech topics suggested on **Handout 84**.

Research Paper Topics

Directions: Choose one of the topics listed below and narrow it. Then choose a second topic and narrow it. Write your topic choices in the space provided.

animals

popular music

video games

hobbies

good nutrition

bike trips

candy making

sports

cars

television shows

environmental problems

airplanes

drug addiction

beauty pageants

clubs

Topic 1: _____

Topic 2: _____

© COPYRIGHT, The Center for Learning. Used with permission. Not for resale.

Name_____

Date_____

Sample Bibliography Entries

Part A.

Directions: Study the following samples of bibliographic note cards.

Sample book entries

Smith, Joe R. *Favorite Dog Breeds.*

1

Sutter, Cheryl. *Dogs Unleashed.*

2

Sample encyclopedia article entry

"American Dogs." *Smart Encyclopedia.*

3

Sample magazine article entry

Johnson, Sam R. *Dog Review.*

4

Part B.

Directions: Study the following example of a finished bibliography.

Bibliography

"American Dogs." *Smart Encyclopedia.*

Johnson, Sam R. *Dog Review.*

Smith, Joe R. *Favorite Dog Breeds.*

Sutter, Cheryl. *Dogs Unleashed.*

© COPYRIGHT, The Center for Learning. Used with permission. Not for resale.

Name_____

Date_____

Research Essay Wheel

Directions: Write your topic in the middle of the wheel. In your own words, write six examples about your topic on the inner spokes. Use two examples from each of your three sources. On the outer spokes, write specific details that support those examples. Refer to your research cards for information to write on the wheel spokes.

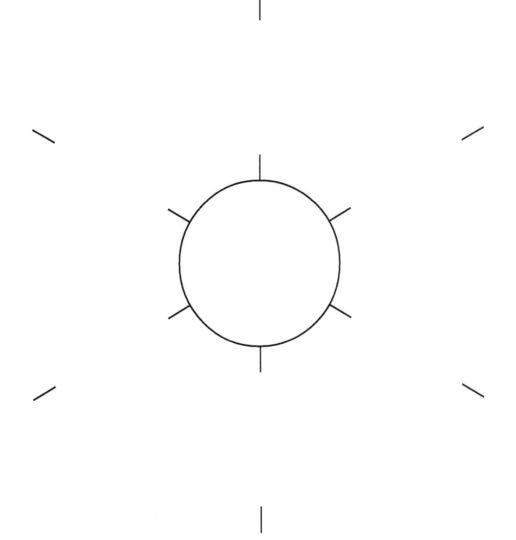

© COPYRIGHT, The Center for Learning. Used with permission. Not for resale.

Name_____

Date_____

Research Essay Writing Chart

Directions: Before you turn in your essay, review this checklist to be sure you have met all the requirements. When you are sure of each item, put a check mark in the student column. Staple this chart to your paper. Your teacher will return this checklist with the items checked that are correct.

Writing Checklist	Student	Teacher
Student indented the paragraph.		
Student followed the formula TS-6EX-SS.		
Student used his or her own words on at least twelve index cards.		
Student used at least three sources.		
Student used a title.		
Student used two transitional words.		
Student used one simile or metaphor.		
Student used three adjectives.		
Student used one onomatopoeia word (optional).		
Student used synonyms.		
Student did not repeat the same noun, adjective, or verb more than three times.		
Student wrote complete sentences.		
Student used at least six to eight words in each sentence.		
Student used the word *because* or another conjunction to write a long sentence.		
Student capitalized the first letter of each sentence.		
Student used correct punctuation at the end of each sentence.		
Student checked spelling.		
Student reread the essay.		

© COPYRIGHT, The Center for Learning. Used with permission. Not for resale.

Lesson 19
Speeches

Objective

- To write and deliver a speech

Notes to the Teacher

Effective speakers do not just read their speeches, they deliver them—hopefully, to an interested audience. Some students like to make speeches if they know how to research and organize what is expected of them. The formula method is an excellent starting point because an informal speech on a specific topic can be organized like a composition. In this lesson, a composition is written and graded before students begin rehearsing it as a speech. Students should be able to speak extemporaneously about their topics if they have done effective research.

Not all students like to give speeches; there are always a few who have a difficult time standing up in front of their classmates. Be sensitive to these students and provide alternative assignments, such as taping a speech ahead of time.

This lesson relies on research skills that are often difficult for elementary students. If the research portion of this lesson is too advanced, it can be omitted. However, the lesson may be simplified to suit students' abilities by

- not requiring students to use index cards for notes
- allowing students to record facts directly on **Handout 85**
- not requiring a written bibliography
- requiring students to use only one source
- decreasing the number of examples in the writing formula

To maximize the effort put into teaching research skills, use the speech/essay assignment to reinforce a topic being studied in science or social studies.

A startling fact from an almanac or encyclopedia is needed for procedure 1. The fact should immediately get your students' attention.

In this lesson, students select a topic, write a one-paragraph essay, and deliver it as a speech. Teachers and students are provided with a speech checklist. Index cards are needed for note taking.

Procedure

1. Write a fact that will startle and interest your students on the board or an overhead transparency. Read the statement aloud. Ask students if you have their attention and why.

   Explain that using a startling fact or statistic is one way speeches begin because it is a good way to get attention. Tell students they will learn other speechmaking techniques in this lesson.

2. Distribute **Handout 84** and have students choose a topic and narrow it. (See procedure 1, Lesson 18.) Topics related to a specific unit can be added. Tell students that they will research the topic, write an essay, and present a speech to the class. Tell the class that the formula method can be used not only to organize their writing, but also their speaking.

3. If necessary, explain to students that a bibliography is an alphabetized list of sources a writer uses when writing a research essay or article; the bibliography is placed at the end of the paper. Tell students that they will be writing a bibliography that includes three sources they used to write their speeches. Have students review **Handout 81** (Lesson 18), sample bibliography entries. Review the format of a bibliography as needed.

4. As needed, review the types of reference materials available at the library. Take students to the library and ask them to do a quick search of their topics. Ask students to draft a working bibliography of at least three different sources for their topic, using **Hand-**

5. When students have three sources, instruct them to record the bibliographic information for the first source on an index card. Students should write a number 1 in the bottom right corner of the index card. Have students complete and number index cards for each entry on their working bibliographies. Tell students that they have just created their bibliographic cards.

6. As needed, review with students how to use index cards to record information they find. (Use their own words to write one idea on each card.) Remind students to include the page number where they found the information. Students should write on the botton right corner of the card the number from the bibliographic card for the source of the information. The cards they have just created are research cards.

   If students find new sources, they should add them to their working bibliographies, create and number a bibliographic card for the source, and use this number on any research cards that use information from the source.

7. Tell students that they should complete at least twelve research cards (a minimum of four research cards from each of three sources of information).

8. When students are done gathering information, instruct them to write a final bibliography. Tell them to arrange their sources in alphabetical order according to the author's last name or the source's title. Ask students to use **Handout 81** as a guide.

9. Have students write their names on the backs of their bibliographic and research cards. Collect the cards and bibliographies to check that students have included enough sources and information. Return the cards and bibliographies to the students.

10. Distribute **Handout 85** and tell students that they will write a one-paragraph essay about their research topic.

    Review the clustering process as needed.
    - Write the topic of the essay in the middle of the wheel.
    - Brainstorm six related ideas for the inner spokes.

    - On the outer spokes, write details that support the examples on the inner spokes.

    Students should refer to their research cards for information.

    Collect, grade, and return **Handout 85** to students.

11. Distribute and review **Handout 86** before students begin writing. You may choose to add other qualifications to the chart. Tell students that when they complete their essays, they should be sure they have met the requirements of each item on the chart, put a check mark in the student column, and stapled the charts to their essays. Explain that you will return the writing chart with the paper after it is graded, with checks in the teacher column for items that are correct.

12. Tell students to review their lists of transitional words, sensory adjectives, and onomatopoeia words. Direct them to complete a synonym chart (**Handout 19**), which they should have in their composition folders.

13. As students begin writing, remind them what the formula TS-6EX-SS means (Topic Sentence—Six Examples—Summary Sentence) and how to use it.
    - Use the words in the middle of the wheel to write a complete topic sentence.
    - Combine the words on each inner spoke with the details on its outer spoke to write six long, complete sentences.
    - Write a summary statement that contains an opinion or a comment about the future.

    Tell students to title their essays with their topic.

14. When students are finished with their paragraphs, tell them to complete the student column on **Handout 86**. Then they should staple **Handouts 19**, **85**, and **86**, the essay, the bibliography, and the bibliographic and research cards together and turn everything in for a grade.

15. Introduce and discuss with the class the following methods of introducing a speech.

A story or anecdote—A personal experience can help the audience to identify with the speaker.

A question—Asking for a response to a question makes the audience feel like it is participating.

A startling fact or statistic—An unusual statement gets the attention of the audience.

A promise—Promising to give your listeners useful information appeals to their needs and interests.

An exhibit—Showing something to the audience helps focus attention.

16. Return graded essays, wheels, writing charts, and index cards and tell students to begin rehearsing their speeches. Students should think of an introduction and visual aids to make their speeches more interesting. Distribute **Handout 87** and review it with the class. Ask students to keep the handout in their composition folders.

17. Distribute **Handout 88,** the chart used to grade speeches. Explain each item on the chart so that students will know the grading criteria before they make their speeches.

18. Allow class time for speeches. Use **Handout 88** to grade each speech. Give the evaluations to students after they have given their speeches.

Name_____

Date_____

Speech Topics

Directions: Pick a topic from the list and narrow it. Write your topic choice in the space provided.

adoption rules

foster care

pollution

sports injuries

current styles and fads

world hunger

homelessness

school uniforms

sports figures

violence in video games

how to study

how to get along with your parents

how to be a friend

motorcycles

smoking hazards

Topic: _____

© COPYRIGHT, The Center for Learning. Used with permission. Not for resale.

Name_____

Date_____

Speech Wheel

Directions: Write your topic in the middle of the wheel. In your own words, write six examples that support your topic on the inner spokes. Use two examples from each of your three sources. Then write details on the outer spokes that support the examples on the inner spokes. Refer to your research index cards for information.

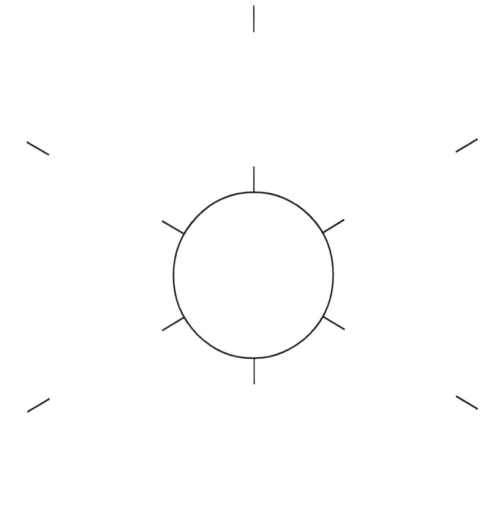

© COPYRIGHT, The Center for Learning. Used with permission. Not for resale.

Name_____

Date_____

Speech Writing Chart

Directions: Before you turn in your essay, review this checklist to be sure you have met all the requirements. When you are sure of each item, put a check mark in the student column. Staple this chart to your paper. Your teacher will return this checklist with the items checked that are correct.

Writing Checklist	Student	Teacher
Student indented the paragraph.		
Student followed the formula TS-6EX-SS.		
Student used his or her own words on at least twelve index cards.		
Student used at least three sources.		
Student used a title.		
Student used two transitional words.		
Student used one simile or metaphor.		
Student used three adjectives.		
Student used one onomatopoeia word.		
Student used synonyms.		
Student did not repeat the same noun, adjective, or verb more than three times.		
Student wrote complete sentences.		
Student used at least six to eight words in each sentence.		
Student used the word *because* or another conjunction to write a long sentence.		
Student capitalized the first letter of each sentence.		
Student used correct punctuation at the end of each sentence.		
Student checked spelling.		
Student reread the essay.		

© COPYRIGHT, The Center for Learning. Used with permission. Not for resale.

Name_____

Date_____

Rules of Speechmaking

Directions: Review these rules so that your speech will be effective. Keep this handout in your composition folder.

1. Follow the essay formula TS-6EX-SS.

2. Show diagrams and pictures.

3. Speak clearly and loudly.

4. Look at your audience.

5. Speak with enthusiasm.

6. Use appropriate facial expressions.

7. Dress appropriately.

8. Stand comfortably.

9. Do not move around, lean, or slouch.

10. Do not chew gum or eat candy.

© COPYRIGHT, The Center for Learning. Used with permission. Not for resale.

Name_____

Date_____

Speech Checklist

Directions: This chart will be used to evaluate your speech.

Student's Name: _____

Speech Checklist	Yes	No
Speaker presented an organized speech according to the formula.		
Speaker added visual aids.		
Speaker spoke clearly.		
Speaker spoke at a good volume.		
Speaker spoke slowly.		
Speaker had good eye contact.		
Speaker spoke with enthusiasm.		
Speaker dressed appropriately.		
Speaker had good posture.		
Speaker was relaxed and confident.		

Grade _____

© COPYRIGHT, The Center for Learning. Used with permission. Not for resale.

Lesson 20
Proofreading

Objective
- To practice proofreading

Notes to the Teacher
Students learn through discovering their mistakes and correcting them. Before they turn their papers in, students need to find and fix mistakes in the items found on the writing charts for each given essay; these charts help students focus on what will be graded and what is important in their papers. The exercises included in this text and exercises found in grammar books should help the teacher with specific problems the students are having. It is now up to the students to take the time and make the effort to look for errors or areas they could change for a specific reason. Having a composition buddy (see Teacher Notes) will help this process. The student's goal is to write the best essay he or she can write.

In this lesson, students cluster and write an essay. They exchange essays with their composition buddies and use an evaluation form to proofread each other's papers. Then students make any needed corrections before turning in their papers.

Procedure
1. Ask students if they like it when someone tells them that they did something incorrectly. (You will probably get a negative response.) After students have had time to respond, ask if it is ever good when someone tells them that they have done something incorrectly. Ask students if they can think of times when people deliberately ask other people to tell them that they've done something incorrectly.

   After they respond, explain to students the concept of proofreading (reading and marking corrections on a piece of writing). Tell students that writers often ask others to proofread their writing, which means they are asking others to tell them if they've written something incorrectly. Writers rely on proofreading because it is often easier for another person to spot mistakes than it is for the writer.

2. Assign a one-paragraph essay using the TS-6EX-SS formula. Simplify one of the following topics or suggest different topics depending on students' abilities.

   - Describe your ideal car.
   - Describe your ideas about how cities will change in the future.
   - Explain what makes an excellent parent.
   - Describe what you like or don't like about autumn.

3. Distribute **Handout 89** and remind students how to cluster.

   - Write the topic of the essay in the middle of the wheel.
   - Brainstorm six related ideas for the inner spokes.
   - On the outer spokes, write details that support the examples on the inner spokes.

4. Distribute and review **Handout 90** before students begin writing. You may choose to add other qualifications to the chart. Tell students that when they complete their essays, they should be sure they have met the requirements of each item on the chart, put a check mark in the student column, and stapled the chart to their essay. Explain that you will return the writing chart with the paper after it is graded, with checks in the teacher column for the items that are correct.

5. Tell students to review their lists of transitional words, sensory adjectives, and onomatopoeia words. Direct them to complete a synonym chart (**Handout 19**), which they should have in their composition folders.

6. As students begin writing, remind them what the formula TS-6EX-SS means (Topic Sentence—Six Examples—Summary Sentence) and how to use it.

   - Use the words in the middle of the wheel to write a complete topic sentence.

   - Combine the words on each inner spoke with the details on its outer spoke to write six long, complete sentences.

   - Write a summary statement that contains an opinion or a comment about the future.

7. When they are finished with their paragraphs, pair students as composition buddies. Distribute **Handout 91** and review it. Direct students to proofread their partner's paper and complete the evaluation form. After both students have read each other's essays, they should exchange evaluation forms. Students should then make any necessary corrections to their papers.

8. When they are finished making proofreading corrections to their papers, tell students to complete the student column on **Handout 90**. Then they should staple **Handouts 19**, **89**, **90**, and **91** to their essay and turn everything in for a grade.

Formula Writing Basics
Lesson 20
Handout 89

Name_____

Date_____

Proofreading Essay Wheel

Directions: Write your topic in the middle of the wheel. Fill the inner spokes with examples about the topic. Then fill the outer spokes with specific details about your examples.

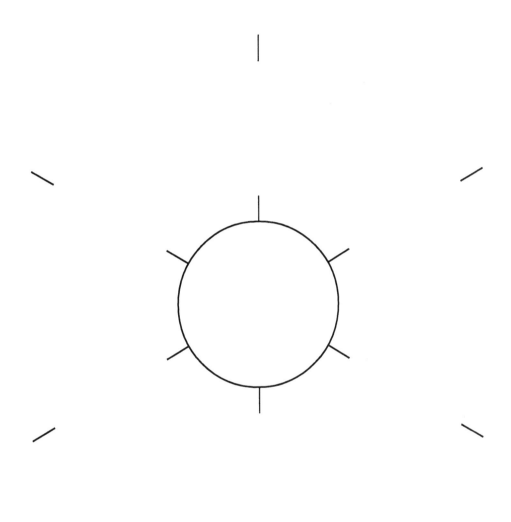

© COPYRIGHT, The Center for Learning. Used with permission. Not for resale.

Name_____

Date_____

Proofreading Essay Writing Chart

Directions: Before you turn in your essay, review this checklist to be sure you have met all the requirements. When you are sure of each item, put a check mark in the student column. Staple this chart to your paper. Your teacher will return this checklist with items checked that are correct.

Writing Checklist	Student	Teacher
Student indented the paragraph.		
Student followed the formula TS-6EX-SS.		
Student used two transitional words.		
Student used one simile or metaphor.		
Student used three adjectives.		
Student used one onomatopoeia word.		
Student used synonyms.		
Student did not repeat the same noun, adjective, or verb more than three times.		
Student wrote complete sentences.		
Student used at least six to eight words in each sentence.		
Student used the word *because* or another conjunction to write a long sentence.		
Student capitalized the first letter of each sentence.		
Student used correct punctuation at the end of each sentence.		
Student checked spelling.		
Student reread the essay.		

© COPYRIGHT, The Center for Learning. Used with permission. Not for resale.

Name_____

Date_____

Evaluation

Directions: Read the essay and make notes of any problems or errors. Then complete this evaluation.

Your Name _____

Author of Composition _____

Questions	Yes	No	Comments
Did the student meet all the requirements of the writing chart?			
Is the essay interesting?			
Does the essay hold the reader's attention?			
Is the essay understandable?			
Is the purpose of the writing clear?			
Are all the ideas and details related to the topic?			
Are the ideas arranged in a logical order?			
Do the ideas flow smoothly?			
Are the words vivid and to the point?			
Is the essay neatly written or printed?			

© COPYRIGHT, The Center for Learning. Used with permission. Not for resale.

Wheel

Directions: Write the topic in the middle of the wheel. Fill the inner spokes with examples of the topic. Then fill the outer spokes with specific details about the examples on the inner spokes.

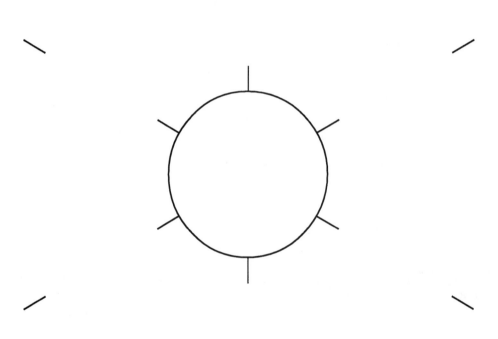

© COPYRIGHT, The Center for Learning. Used with permission. Not for resale.

Name_____

Date_____

Writing Chart

Directions: Before you turn in your paper, review this checklist to be sure you have met all the requirements. When you are sure of each item, put a check mark in the student column. Staple this chart to your paper. Your teacher will put check marks in the teacher column for what is correct.

Writing Checklist	Student	Teacher
Student indented the paragraph.		
Student followed the formula TS-6EX-SS.		
Student wrote complete sentences.		
Student used at least six to eight words in each sentence.		
Student capitalized the first letter of each sentence.		
Student used correct punctuation at the end of each sentence.		
Student checked spelling.		
Student reread the essay.		

© COPYRIGHT, The Center for Learning. Used with permission. Not for resale.

Name_____

Date_____

Clustering Steps

1. Write the topic of the essay in the middle of the wheel.

2. Brainstorm six related ideas for the inner spokes.

3. On the outer spokes, write details that support the examples on the inner spokes.

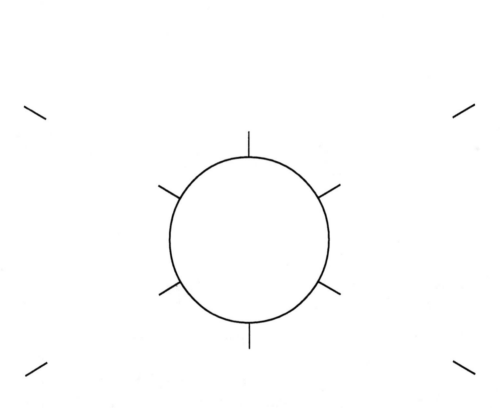

© COPYRIGHT, The Center for Learning. Used with permission. Not for resale.

Name_____

Date_____

Writing Steps

1. Use the words in the middle of the wheel to write a complete topic sentence.

2. Combine the words on each inner spoke with the details on its outer spoke to write six long, complete sentences.

3. Write a summary statement that contains an opinion or a comment about the future.

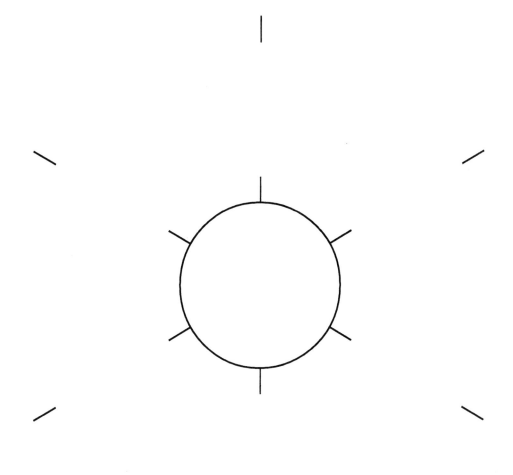

© COPYRIGHT, The Center for Learning. Used with permission. Not for resale.

Language Arts Series

Advanced Placement

Advanced Placement English:
Practical Approaches to Literary Analysis

Advanced Placement English:
In-depth Analysis of Literary Forms

Advanced Placement Poetry

Advanced Placement Short Story

Advanced Placement Writing 1

Advanced Placement Writing 2

Composition

Advanced Composition

Basic Composition

Creative Writing

Daily Writing Topics

Formula Writing Basics—Beginning a Writing
Proficiency Program

Formula Writing 1—Building Toward Writing
Proficiency

Formula Writing 2—Diverse Writing Situations

Grammar Mastery—For Better Writing,
Workbook Level 1

Grammar Mastery—For Better Writing,
Workbook Level 2

Grammar Mastery—For Better Writing,
Teacher Guide

Grammar Power—the Essential Elements,
Student Workbook

Grammar Power—the Essential Elements,
Teacher Guide

Journalism: Writing for Publication

Research 1: Information Literacy

Research 2: The Research Paper

Writing 1: Learning the Process

Writing 2: Personalizing the Process

Writing Short Stories

Writing Skills and the Job Search

Genres

Mythology

Nonfiction: A Critical Approach

Participating in the Poem

Science Fiction—19th Century

Short Poems: Their Vitality and Versatility

The Short Story

Thematic Approaches to British Poetry

Literary Traditions

American Literature 1:
Beginnings through Civil War

American Literature 2:
Civil War to Present

Archetypes in Life, Literature, and Myth

British Literature 1:
Beginnings to Age of Reason

British Literature 2: Romantics to the Present

Honors American Literature 1

Honors American Literature 2

Multicultural Literature:
Essays, Fiction, and Poetry

World Literature 1

World Literature 2

Skills

Creative Dramatics in the Classroom

Junior High Language Arts

Speech

Thinking, Reading, Writing, Speaking

Special Topic

Supervisor/Student Teacher Manual

Peer Mediation: Training Students in Conflict
Resolution

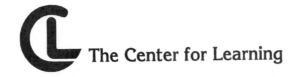

The Center for Learning

The Publisher

All instructional materials identified by the TAP® (Teachers/Authors/Publishers) trademark are developed by a national network of teachers whose collective educational experience distinguishes the publishing objective of The Center for Learning, a nonprofit educational corporation founded in 1970.

Concentrating on values-related disciplines, The Center publishes humanities and religion curriculum units for use in public and private schools and other educational settings. Approximately 500 language arts, social studies, novel/drama, life issues, and faith publications are available.

While acutely aware of the challenges and uncertain solutions to growing educational problems, The Center is committed to quality curriculum development and to the expansion of learning opportunities for all students. Publications are regularly evaluated and updated to meet the changing and diverse needs of teachers and students. Teachers may offer suggestions for development of new publications or revisions of existing titles by contacting

The Center for Learning

Administrative/Editorial Office
21590 Center Ridge Road
Rocky River, Ohio, 44116
(440) 331-1404 • FAX (440) 331-5414
E-mail: cfl@stratos.net
Web: http://www.centerforlearning.org

For a free catalog containing order and price information and a descriptive listing of titles, contact

The Center for Learning

Shipping/Business Office
P.O. Box 910
Villa Maria, PA 16155
(724) 964-8083 • (800) 767-9090
FAX (888) 767-8080